Secret Doors
of the
Qabala

Other Ted Andrews Titles

Books Through Dragonhawk Publishing

Treasures of the Unicorn
Music Therapy for Non-Musicians
More Simplified Magic
Psychic Protection
The Animal-Wise Tarot
Animal-Wise
Magic of Believing
Psychic Power
Spirits, Ghosts and Guardians
Faerie Charms
The Animal-Speak Workbook
Nature-Speak
The Art of Shapeshifting
The Occult Christ (revised edition)
The Nature-Speak Oracle

Books Through Llewellyn Publications

Simplified Qabala Magic
Imagick
Sacred Power in Your Name
How To See and Read the Aura
The Magickal Name
Dream Alchemy
How to Uncover Past Lives
Sacred Sounds
How to Meet and Work with Spirit Guides
How to Heal with Color
Magickal Dance
Enchantment of the Faerie Realm
Animal-Speak
The Healer's Manual
How to Develop Psychic Touch
Crystal Balls and Crystal Bowls

Books Through Hampton Roads Publishing

Dreamsong of the Eagle

Spoken-Audio through Life Magic Enterprises, Inc.

Roses of Light
Uncover Your Past Lives
Mystery of the Fire Spirits
Upon the Wings of Angels
Psychic Protection
Discover Your Spirit Animal
Entering the Tree of Life

Secret Doors
of the
Qabala

by

Ted Andrews

Dragonhawk Publishing   Jackson, Tennessee

A Dragonhawk Publishing Book

Secret Doors of the Qabala

First Edition

Book design by Ted Andrews

ISBN 13: 978-1-888767-49-0

Library of Congress Catalog Card Number: 2004115577

This book was designed and produced
by Dragonhawk Publishing
Jackson, TN
USA

*my cat is a master of mind control,
therefore I cannot be held
responsible for the following:*

*Alladin,
&
Ichabod*

Table of Contents

Table of Contents

Part IV - Secret of Dancing the Tree

Part V - Secret of the Hidden Paths

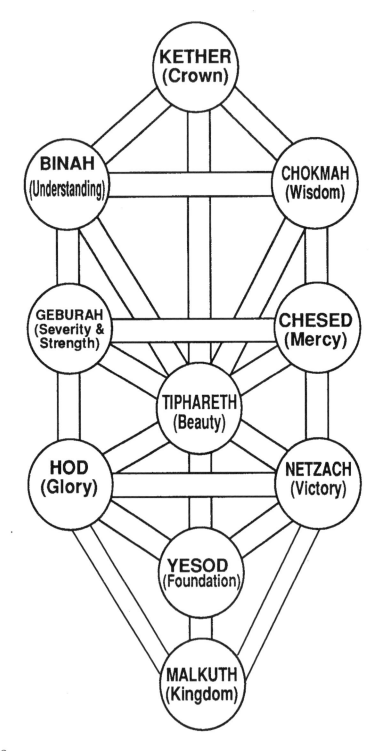

Introduction

Magic
of the Qabala

I was always a voracious reader. Throughout most of my childhood, the local library had a limit on the number of books you could check out at any one time and you had to return them within two weeks. I would always check out the limit and always have them read within three to four days. One of my happiest moments was when the library gave me special permission to check out more books than they normally allowed. On one of these occasions, I read a book of short stories and in it was the tale of a group of men. These men used something called the Kaballah to create a monster out of mud to save themselves from the Nazis.

Since that time the Qabala (regardless of its spelling: Kaballah, Cabala, etc.) has always held a great fascination for me. The word resonated with a part of me in a mysterious and haunting way. I grew up in a time in which metaphysical writings (outside of a traditional religious context) were not readily available. I could always find some astrology and yoga, and although the yoga did not appeal to me, I was able to teach myself how to erect an astrological chart in high school – including doing the necessary math. (Yes, this was long before computers took all of the tedious labor out of it.)

Then I found a bookstore downtown that began to carry esoteric books (as they were called then). They were stuck in the farthest back corner, away from everything "normal". It was a hodge-podge of literature that did not fit any other category from the erotic to the metaphysical. It was here that I always looked for more information on the mystical and psychic realm, especially on that strange thing called Qabala.

I would buy any book that even had anything resembling it in its titles or between the covers. Now at that time, most of the information on Qabala was either so vague or esoteric that no normal person could understand it or it assumed you already had a working knowledge of it. And there certainly weren't any teachers around for it. It wouldn't be until my freshman year of college that I began to explore its meaning and experiment with ways of incorporating it into my own meditations and psychic development.

It was then that the dream came. This dream would become the key to truly understanding and applying the magic of the Qabala to normal everyday life. This dream helped me to realize that the most powerful things in the world are often the most simple. Part of this dream became the introductory story found in what would be my very first book, *Simplified Magic – a Beginner's Guide to the New Age Qabala* or as its titled in its newest edition *Simplified Qabala Magic*. Through this dream, I found that the Qabala didn't have to be as complicated as so many often made it.

I would eventually discover in the Qabala a practical system for awakening the qualities necessary to accelerate spiritual growth. I found a system of spiritual and magical unfoldment that is safe and practical. I found a system that enables the exploration of our highest potentials and opens new dimensions without overwhelming us in the process.

Whether developing psychic abilities, walking a healing path, exploring spirit dimensions, connecting with totems and Nature or communicating with angels, the ancient and mystical Qabala is a map that allows us to do so more safely and more powerfully. It enables us to develop our greatest potentials and face our greatest weaknesses.

Contrary to what many believe today, the purpose of spiritual studies is not for psychic power. Rather, it is for the ability to look beyond physical limitations, to learn the creative possibilities that exist within limitations, while at the same time transcending them. The purpose of spiritual studies is to help us rediscover the wonder, awe and power of the divine and to learn how that power reveals and reflects itself within each of us and our lives.

The ancient Qabala is a timeless map that allows us to look into ourselves for our answers – for our magic and our miracles. Not from books or from teachers – although they serve their purposes – but from the well of truth that lies within. The Qabala teaches us that the spiritual path is not a path that leads up to some divine light into which all of our troubles are dissolved. Rather it teaches us how to awaken the light within, so that we may shine it out from us.

The Tree of Life

The mystical Qabala is one of the most ancient of all the mystery traditions. There exists much argument over its true origin, as does the origin of any oral teaching tradition. Qabala comes from the words *qibel* which means "to receive" or "that which is received", and it is aligned with those mystical teaching that were only passed down through word of mouth.

The Qabala is rich in powerful symbolism. Almost every major civilization has utilized aspects of the Qabala and its primary image, the Tree of Life. Most of what comes down to us today retains strong threads to the ancient Egyptian and Hebrew traditions. As will be seen, it is not necessary for us to be fluent in Egyptian or Hebrew or any of the ancient languages and traditions to understand and work with the Qabala.

At the heart of the Qabalistic teachings is the diagram of the Tree of Life. It is a diagram to the treasures of the universe - magical and material. It is a symbol rich in rewards for those who have the keys to unlocking it. These keys are part of what this book will provide.

The Tree of Life diagram can be viewed from different perspectives. For our purposes, we will examine it from two. The first deals more with the philosophy and cosmology, while the second relates more to pragmatic applications. Most of our focused work will be connected to the second.

On one level, the Tree of Life symbol depicts how the universe was formed. The universe issued forth out of what is called *NOTHINGNESS* - the Ain Soph - some primal point from which we came and to which we will return. While we are in the physical, we can know little or nothing about it, and thus it is called NOTHINGNESS.

The universe came forth out of the Nothingness and underwent nine stages of manifestation - nine stages of compacting, condensing and channeling of divine energy - to manifest in a tenth stage encompassing the entire material universe - all matter and life upon the Earth. This can be loosely compared to the process of condensing steam into water and then into ice. It is still two parts hydrogen and one part oxygen, but it has condensed into solid matter. The universe, including ourselves, is spiritual, divine energy that has condensed into physical matter. This process of manifestation into material being is known as *The Path of the Flaming Sword.*

There is much more to the Tree of Life than meets the eye. It reflects more than just the process that the universe underwent to come into being. It is also a map to the human mind. It is a map through the labyrinth of the subconscious. The subconscious mind controls over 90% of the body's functions, and it has many levels within it. Each level of the subconscious is tied to and/or controls different physiological functions, different organs and different abilities. And each level of the subconscious is related to a level on the Tree of Life. Awakening the Tree of

Life and all of its inherent energies with us is essential to both the magical and mystical existence. It requires that we consciously stimulate our perceptions in both the physical and non-physical environments.

THE PATH OF THE FLAMING SWORD

NOTHINGNESS—Primal Point from which we came and to which we return, beyond understanding.

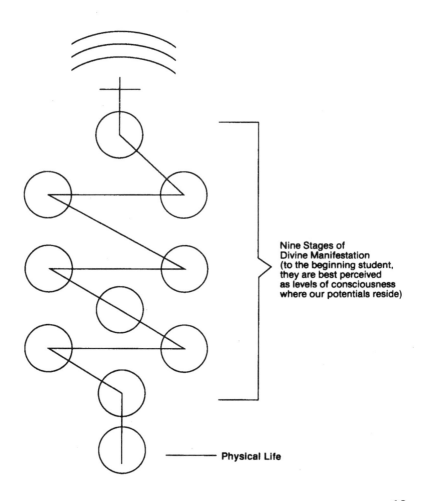

Nine Stages of Divine Manifestation (to the beginning student, they are best perceived as levels of consciousness where our potentials reside)

Physical Life

Mysticism of the Tree

The tree is an ancient symbol. It represents things that grow. It represents fertility and life. To some, it is the world axis, and to others it is the world itself. Its roots are within the earth, and yet it reaches to the sky. It is a bridge between the heavens and the earth; the mediator between both worlds. This is most reflective of the Qabala and its application to our entire unfoldment process. Through it we work to bridge one level of our consciousness with the next, just as the tree bridges the heavens and the earth.

The tree, as the Tree of Knowledge, has been associated with both Paradise and Hell. In Greek mythology the Golden Fleece hung upon a tree. The Christian cross was originally a tree, and Buddha found enlightenment while sitting beneath one. Druids recognized the energies and spirits of trees, while the Norse honored Yggdrasil, the Tree of Life. Every civilization and traditions has its stories, myths and mystical legends of trees.

Trees bear fruit from which we gain nourishment. They provide shade and shelter. The wood is essential to the building of homes, and it is also essential to the making of paper - a source for communication and knowledge. The leaves of many trees fall in the autumn only to re-emerge again in the spring, reflecting the continual change and growth - the dying only to be reborn. We rake the leaves in the autumn, gathering what has dropped to create mulch for future plantings. Trees also serve as barriers, often used as a windbreak or fence by farmers. They are boundaries, whether separating one piece of land from another or one world from another.

Trees have always been imbued with certain magical and spiritual attributes. The superstition of "knocking on wood" originated as practice to ensure no spirits were in a tree before it was cut down and thus inadvertently upsetting the spirits. In German folklore, the kobolde were spirits inhabiting trees. When these trees were cut, a piece of the tree was carved into a figure so that the spirit would always have a place to live. These carvings were shut up in wooden boxes and brought inside of the house. Only the owner was permitted to open it, and if anyone else did, the result would be untold damage. Children were warned not to go near them, and jack-in-the-boxes were fashioned to scare kids and remind them not to touch the real boxes.

Most people are familiar with the family tree. This tree has its roots in our ancestors, both familial and spiritual. All that we are lies in the roots of the tree, and thus all of our ancestry can be awakened through the tree. There are exercises that we can do with the tree of life to reveal ancestors and past lives that have helped create and nurture the tree we are now.

Secret Magic of the Qabala

Magic is one of the most misunderstood terms in metaphysical and spiritual studies. Magic is not some form of hocus pocus or prestidigitation. It is not burning candles and casting spells. Neither is it mere divination or pacts with spiritual beings of any sort. At its root, it means "wisdom", and to enter into its practice without the appropriate reverence, respect and understanding will lead to many problems down the road.

MAGIC is a divine process, based upon wisdom. It is the expression of wisdom. It is a means to an end. It is the development of mastery over life (or aspects of life) with the expression of that mastery within our everyday activities. Anyone who has mastered some aspect of life can be viewed as a magician. Being able to handle conflicts with patience, tolerance and insight can seem magickal to many people. To someone who knows nothing about plumbing, a plumber's ability to effect repairs is magical.

Magic is the application of knowledge, understanding and wisdom to life. It is discovering that the Divine already exists within us. It is discovering that life is supposed to go right. It is discovering how to make it right. It is amazing how often I hear people exclaim, "The most amazing thing just happened!" when they receive answers to their prayers of experience miraculous and magickal happenings within their lives.

The truth is that prayers are supposed to be answered. Miracles and magic are supposed to happen. It would be truly amazing if they did not occur. It is our own doubts, fears, recriminations, sense of unworthiness, and refusal to look beyond our limited perspectives that delay and hinder the manifestation of a magically wonderful existence.

Magic is one path in the quest for the spirit, the search for that innermost part, the point of our greatest reality. As with all spiritual paths, it is not a path that leads up to some Divine light into which all of our troubles are dissolved or from which there is no return. It is a path to finding the Divine Light within so that we can shine it forth.

The Qabala is rich is mystical symbols and images. As we will learn, these symbols and images are magical tools that we can use to link our consciousness to other levels, planes and beings. By learning to use them in a controlled and directed manner, we can manifest their energies in such a dynamic manner that we become living, loving examples of the highest and best. We become living beings of light. This constitutes a true alchemical change. This awakens the higher self in a fully conscious manner.

In order to accomplish this most effectively, we need to understand five secrets of the Qabala. Opening the doors to these secrets is the key to opening the doors to our greatest potentials. These five secrets create a sacred pentagram and all of them are explored in this book with special emphasis on the last two. These secret doors to the Qabala help us to open to our greatest potentials. These five secrets are:

1. The secret of magickal images and symbols.
2. The secret of Daath

3. The secret of pathworking
4. The secret of dancing the tree of life.
5. The secret of the hidden paths.

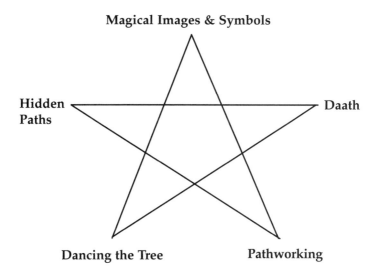

Magical Images & Symbols

Hidden Paths

Daath

Dancing the Tree

Pathworking

There are those who may scoff at my approach to the Qabala, but I have always been very pragmatic toward everything psychic, spiritual, and metaphysical. Show me that if I do such and such that I can expect discernable, predictable and tangible results. This book is designed with exercises that will elicit recognizable, tangible results in a rather quick and often surprising manner. As they used to say, "The proof is in the pudding." This is why I have always loved Qabala and I always fall back on it.

In the year after my first book, *Simplified Magic - A Beginner's Guide to the New Age Qabala*, was released, I received some very interesting mail from major occult and metaphysical groups/societies in different parts of the world. Several of these occult and magical societies condemned me for putting the information on the Qabala out to the general public in a way that was accessible to everyone. It was irresponsible of me.

Although some condemned me for writing a simple book on Qabala, these letters were a confirmation that I had done the right thing. For too long, groups tended to keep sacred knowledge in their own hands - often under the guise that the average person was not able to handle it. Most of the time though, this reasoning was simply a way of trying to maintain a false position of spiritual power.

If I have learned nothing else in the past 35 years of working and teaching in this field, it is that humans are capable of understanding and handling much more than with what we are often credited. We are beings of great potential, light and wonder, and Qabala is a path to help us uncover the sacredness that is our true essence. And these secret doors will help you to shine a little more brightly within your life.

Part I -

The Secret
of
Magical Images

Chapter One

The Secret of Magical Images

A multitude of methods, tools and techniques exist for awakening our innermost energies and potentials. Most of these though do little more than just that. They simply awaken. For many people, this is comparable to stirring up a hornet's nest. Energy awakened inappropriately (especially when ill prepared) results in chaos. Energy unused or misused once awakened becomes disruptive.

Although there are lessons we can learn from chaos and disruption, there are much easier ways of learning. I am a firm believer that suffering is only good for the soul if it teaches us how not to suffer in that way again. The key is knowing how to absorb and integrate the energy awakened. As we will discover with the Qabala, this is accomplished through creative imagination and the use of magical images.

Most methods for awakening our potentials and for accessing the universal and spiritual energies of life fall into one of two categories: **meditative** and **ceremonial.** One is neither better nor worse than the other. Both include the use of symbology, visualization, creative imagination, pathworking, mantras, yantras, and many other tools to awaken the universal energies. The primary difference is that ceremonial methods often involve more intricately ritualized physical activities.

The Qabala employs both kinds, but this book will focus more upon the ceremonial techniques and tools. The magical techniques throughout this work are created to elicit very specific results. They will allow you to experience the power of the Qabala and to use it more effectively. They will enable you to increasingly manifest the universal forces more tangibly into your daily life, without being overwhelmed by them.

Planting Seeds with Images & Symbols

With every meditation, with every magical working, we are planting a seed thought. Planting a seed thought means placing a clear magical or mystical idea or image into our visualizations with strong intention. This consigns the seed thought or image to the subconscious mind, where it will begin to grow and increase in energy on its own. If we repeat this process every day, if only for a few moments, the magical idea, image and/or working will become a bridge to the Divine world by awakening our innermost potentials. At the very least, it energizes our entire life, increases our creativity and enhances our expression of life while in the physical.

The symbols and images associated with the Qabalistic Tree of Life are tools for opening doors beyond the realm of our physical environment. Qabala provides a system of using these symbols and images to explore the more subtle realms without getting lost. It provides a powerful how-to for almost any image and symbol.

Symbols and images are guideposts. In the Qabala, certain ones have been used in a similar fashion by many people for many centuries, thus the paths are already laid out for us, with built in markers to prevent our getting lost. All we need to do is learn to read the markers and walk the paths in order to link our energy with the universal energy activated by this work with the images and symbols.

Empowering our life through the Qabalistic symbols, images and seed thoughts requires understanding the language of symbols, and then it requires setting up the conditions that cause a mental shift to a new way of processing information - an altered state of consciousness.

Through the techniques in this book, we learn to use the language of symbols to delve into parts of our mind that are too often obscured by the endless details of daily life. Through proper use of Qabalistic symbols, images and seed thoughts, we can create a mind-set that perceives life in a new manner. We begin to see underlying patterns, and we access our greater potentials and release them into our normal consciousness. We discover solutions to problems and we add energy and animation to our lives.

In working with the Tree of Life, we are consciously learning how to to tap energies represented and reflected through them. Each sephira - each level of consciousness - is a temple in which specific energies are more available to us. These energies are translated to and awakened within us through symbols and images.

The colors, names, letters, tarot associations, astrological glyphs and all of the other images and symbols associated with each level of the Tree of Life are links to universal powers that play in and through us through the

DRAWING UPON THE SUBCONSCIOUS

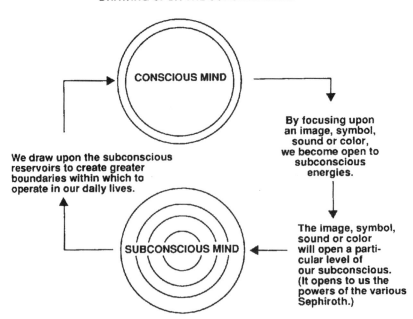

CONSCIOUS MIND

By focusing upon an image, symbol, sound or color, we become open to subconscious energies.

We draw upon the subconscious reservoirs to create greater boundaries within which to operate in our daily lives.

SUBCONSCIOUS MIND

The image, symbol, sound or color will open a particular level of our subconscious. (It opens to us the powers of the various Sephiroth.)

specific levels of our subconscious mind. Understanding the Tree of Life helps us understand the energy within us.

Something as simple as color and fragrance will open the doors of our subconscious mind that correspond to specific levels or sephiroth on the Tree of Life with all of their inherent energies. They ring the doorbell of specific levels of our mind, and then the other magical images and symbols trigger responses awakening the potentials that have been dormant within us.

The magical images and symbols associated with a sephira that we have stimulated through the use of color and fragrance then help us to access and express those energies more directly and consciously in our daily life. The formula is simple:

Candle & Fragrance Reference Chart

Sephira	Color of Candle	Fragrances
Kether	white	frankincense, ambergris
Chokmah	gray	eucalyptus, musk, geranium
Binah	black	myrrh, chamomile
Chesed	blue	bayberry, cedar, nutmeg
Geburah	red	cinnamon, tobacco, cypress
Tiphareth	yellow	rose, jasmine, lily
Netzach	green	patchouli, rose, bayberry
Hod	orange	rosemary, frangipani, mints
Yesod	violet	wisteria, lavender, honeysuckle
Malkuth	citrine, olive russet or black	sandalwood, lemon, carnation

Opening the subconscious mind
+
Stimulating dormant energies & potentials =

Freeing & manifesting greater powers

In essence, we are taking an intangible expression of energy and potential within us and giving it a tangible representation through the symbol or image. In this way we activate its influence upon us more dynamically and in turn, we can manifest and express those energies more effectively within our lives.

To achieve results, to tap deeper levels of consciousness and to manifest our innermost powers, we need only to learn how to shift our awareness in the appropriate manner and then maintain it for the time and purpose necessary. This is a learned skill! The Qabala provides all of the tools (often in the form of images and symbols) necessary to accomplish this, and the more we use them, the more energy, power and magic manifests within our lives. *This is the first and most important secret of the magical Qabala.*

Qabalistic symbols and images help us access forces and energies latent within us and the universe. They open doors to ever-deepening levels of consciousness and perception. The images, symbols and correspondences of the Tree of Life are ways of controlling specific aspects and manifestations of archetypal force within our lives.

Most effective occult techniques are very simple. They depend upon capacities that can be developed by any intelligent man or woman. Yes, depth of control requires much more time and energy, but *everyone* can achieve some results almost immediately. When we use symbols, images and seed thoughts to develop controlled creative imagination and then use that creative imagination to give birth to our true essence, our life takes a quantum leap. We become the living Tree of Life!

Tapping Hidden Levels
Through Symbols & Images

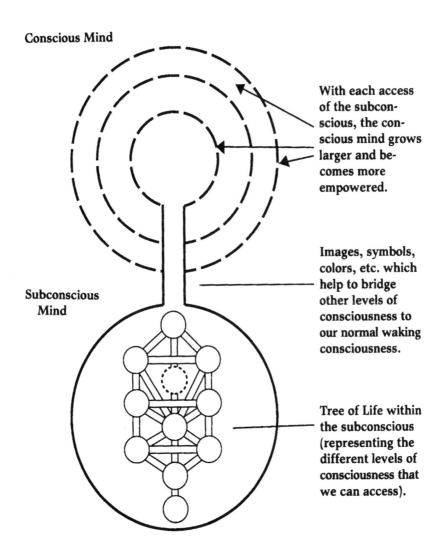

Conscious Mind

With each access of the subconscious, the conscious mind grows larger and becomes more empowered.

Subconscious Mind

Images, symbols, colors, etc. which help to bridge other levels of consciousness to our normal waking consciousness.

Tree of Life within the subconscious (representing the different levels of consciousness that we can access).

Magical Symbology

Symbology is the language of the unconscious, and each of us at some point will need to learn more about it and how to use it to our fullest capability. If we intend to step out on the path of controlled evolution, we must become aware of the power and significance of symbols within our lives.

To understand symbols is to understand ourselves. They help us to understand what our beliefs, superstitions, fears are based upon. They can also open us to levels of our being that we have either ignored or been unaware of. Symbols span the world of thought and the world of being. They provide a means of understanding and interacting with the true world of hidden realities within us and our life. They express what we have no words for.

Symbols bridge the rational and intuitive levels of our being. They lead us from the limited regions of the conscious mind to the unlimited regions of the subconscious mind. They touch both objective and subjective realities. They are a means for the subconscious to send forth information to the conscious mind that might not have discerned it otherwise. They bridge the finite aspects of us with our more infinite potentials.

Good guided imagery and symbols are derived from archetypes and thus at some point in our use of them, they lead us back to those archetypes. The archetypes are the manifesting energies of the universe. The archetypes are the points where the abstract divine forces begin to take upon themselves more substantial forms of expression. If we do not attempt to work with the archetypes and clear the debris from our life, we will not progress beyond a certain point. The symbols and images assist us in merging our finite mind with the infinite mind of the universe.

Symbology and imagery are a part of our essence and have tremendous spiritual import to us. They are accumulators of energy which, if used properly, release archetypal forces to play out within our lives. The techniques of this book are designed to teach how to use symbols and images of the Qabala for the greater activation and control of archetypal energies in all areas of our life. In this way we discover that we can truly change our world.

Understanding the relation between the archetypal forces of the universe and the symbols and images that bridge them into our daily lives is critical to leading a magical existence. At the core of every symbol and image lies some archetypal force. Energy translated from the archetypal to the sensible ones of physical life take the form of images and symbols in order for us to recognize them and work with them. Likewise, it requires proper use of symbols and images to connect back to the archetypal forces. This is why the Tree of Life places such an invaluable role in unfolding our potentials. It provides the tools for working with them properly.

Through the Tree of Life we learn to use images as a carpenter uses wood, hammer and saw. Qabalistic images and symbols are the tools we use to build perception of the spiritually creative worlds and their energies playing within our lives. This means we must be able to construct a passive, reflected thought or image and then transform that thought through our *creative imagination* into a living, empowered energy. When we can accomplish this, we can consciously open the doors, communicate and interact with all of the spiritual realms.

A physically and spiritually creative person is one who can process information in new ways. A creative individual intuitively sees possibilities for transforming ordinary data and everyday experiences into new creations. It is an individual who can see the creative possibilities that exist in limitations. To accomplish this, we must be able to learn in new ways.

Inside each of our skulls we have a double brain with two ways of knowing and learning. The different characteristics of the two hemispheres of the brain have a dynamic role in releasing higher potentials into our daily life expression - especially when working together.

Each of the hemispheres gathers in the same sensory information, but they handle that information in different ways. One hemisphere (often the dominant left in Western society) will inhibit the other half. The left hemisphere analyzes, counts, marks time, plans and views logically and in a step-by-step procedure. It verbalizes, makes statements and draws conclusions based on logic. It is sequential and linear in its approach to life.

On the other hand, we do have a second way of knowing and learning. This is known as right-brain activity. We see things that may be imaginary - existing only in the mind's eye - or recall things that may be real. We see how things exist in space and how parts go together to make a whole. Through it we understand metaphors, we dream and we create new combinations of ideas. Through the right hemisphere we tap and use intuition and have leaps of insight - moments when everything seems to fall into place but not in a logical manner. The intuitive, subjective, relational, wholistic and the time-free mode is right hemisphere activity.

One of the marvelous capacities of the right hemisphere is imaging, *seeing an image or picture with the mind's eye.* The brain is able to conjure an image and then hold it and work with it. These images reflect our sensory information and data - past, present and future. Something imagined is not something unreal. It is simply a product of the imaging faculty of the brain that has a source, even if unidentified.

Because of this faculty, symbols, visualization and creative imagination are often a part of developing higher potentials. The symbols and images assist us in accessing that part of our brain and mind which bridges into deeper levels of perception and consciousness. Learning to use the right brain to tap and access specific level of consciousness in a balanced and fully conscious manner - to bring it out and then apply it to some aspect of our daily lives - involves hemispheric synchronization - working with both sides of the brain.

The Qabala teaches us how to do this. It provides an organized system of images to access and connect deeper levels of our subconscious mind to our normal waking consciousness. It is a system (left brain) of image and symbol usage (right brain). Our unfoldment becomes a safer and easier process when we control and work through a balanced system. By working with such a system in an appropriate manner, we use both sides of our brain and more fully tap our subconscious - which opens all the doorways to our intuitive, higher self.

When we control, direct and focus the inner energies consciously, we are doing what the teacher and mystic Rudolph Steiner referred to as "grabbing the serpent of wisdom by the neck". We are choosing and directing the movement of energy within ourselves and our lives. We do it consciously and with full responsibility. We learn to make the energies work for us when we wish and how we wish.

The key to empowering our life is setting up conditions that create a mental shift to a new way of processing information. Through the techniques in this book, we will learn to delve into parts of the mind and its perceptions that are often obscured by the endless details of daily life. Through the proper use of images and symbols, we create a mind-set that begins the process of unveiling the hidden to us. We begin to see underlying patterns, and we access greater potentials and manifest them within our daily lives.

Reflections of the Divine in You

We are physical beings. This means our primary focus should be within the physical world, but we can use other dimensions and levels of consciousness to create more productivity within our physical lives. If we are to use other, deeper levels of consciousness for our betterment, then we need to transform the energy potentials of the inner to the outer life. It is the magical body that assists us with this. With each touching of the sephiroth, we release energy that assists in molding, creating and empowering the ideal self - the true magical person that lives within us. The magical body is a reflection of our inherent divinity.

Associated with each sephira is a magical image and magical gifts. This magical image is a tremendously powerful thought form that has been created through constant work on the Tree of Life through the ages. Tapping these thought forms assists us in creating our own variations and expressions of the energy represented and reflected by the image. The magical gift reflects the divine power inherent within you that we are trying to manifest.

These magical images and gifts reflect a tangible expression of the more abstract energies available to us through that level of our consciousness. In touching each level, we assimilate the energies of the magical image into ourselves. This in turn enables us to more fully tap and use the energies of the Tree of Life more fully within our daily lives. It makes it easier to manifest the energies associated with the gift. The magical images help us move from merely developing a magical body to becoming a very real magical being.

This book is about working with images of the Tree of Life - paths and sephiroth - and learning secret and powerful ways how to enter into them in a sympathetic manner. To do so, we must be able to loosen the restrictions of the mind. Any creative person, artist or inventor has already learned to do so. Through the use of *Secret Doors of the Qabala* we are learning to use the imagination in a productive manner. We are developing the ability to see the significance and interrelatedness of all things. Such skills take time and practice, but once accomplished, they grant us power, strength and control over our life and destiny.

Magical Images and Gifts

Sephira	Magical Image	Magical Gift
Kether	ancient, bearded king, seen in profile	spinning top
Chokmah	bearded male	scepter of power
Binah	mature woman, matron	black cloak of concealament
Chesed	mighty throned king	cornucopia
Geburah	warrior in chariot	sword
Tiphareth	king, sacrificed god & a child	crown too large
Netzach	beautiful naked woman	rose
Hod	hermaphrodite	caduceus pendant
Yesod	beautiful naked man	silver slippers, mirror
Malkuth	young maiden, crowned and throned	grains, gems, sacred oils

Keep in mind that there will always be elements that we cannot control as long as we are in the physical. This play of free variables in life is what forces us to become ever more creative and productive. Through the proper use of magical images and symbols, we become more active within our life. We unfold our own power and magic. We realize that we can take a more creative and active role in our life circumstances. Working with the symbols and images of the Tree of Life helps us with this.

The Tree of Life in Body and Mind

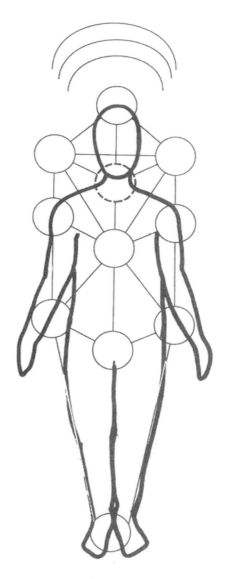

The Tree of Life can be associated with parts of the universe, parts of the body, and levels of the mind as well. Each Sephira corresponds to a particular level of the subconscious through which archetypal energies manifest and find expression in our life. Learning to tap those levels helps us to understand and control more of what happens in our life.

Chapter Two

Entering the Tree of Life

The process of using symbols and images to tap and bridge deeper levels of our consciousness is what the Qabala entails. It helps us to consciously align to corresponding powers of the universe and link them with our normal state of mind. Such a process involves dynamic visualization, meditation and/or physical activities in a prescribed manner according to natural principles. They build a bridge between the inner worlds and the outer world in which we operate. They link the spiritual and the physical, creating a flow between them that augments our energies, abilities and potentials in all areas of our life.

The images and correspondences within the Qabala are effective because they have been used in a manner similar to that described for many hundreds of years. The effects of working with these symbols and images upon the day to day life are very definable because they have been used in such similar fashions with such similar results.

By focusing upon a particular image, color or symbol, we stimulate a specific level of the subconscious. It awakens it and its untapped potentials, opening us to our innate abilities and to spiritual forces outside of us to which we have access. We use the Qabalistic images to open and activate the subconscious mind's reservoirs and abilities. We expand the conscious boundaries within which they can operate in our daily lives. Their energies not only become more available to us, but we become more aware of their influence within our life circumstances as well.

Through the Qabalistic images and symbols we can set energy in motion on higher, more subtle planes of life. These in turn trigger a corresponding action or effect within our physical, daily lives. Learning these images and symbols and how to use them to create magickal effects within our life is what this book entails. This is just one of the five secret doors of the true magical Qabala.

Tree of Life & the Subconscious Mind

Each of the ten stages or levels, known as Sephiroth in the Qabala, represents a level of the subconscious mind - a level of consciousness to which we have access. They are temples of the mind. Each temple or level of consciousness has its own gifts and its own unique benefits - from controlling physiological functions to stimulating artistic energies to communicating with animals and more. Through each level we can connect more fully with a specific aspect of the Divine. Through each level, we can connect and communicate with a specific archangel and group of angelic beings. Through each level, we can experience and understand specific astrological influences within our life.

Through work with the Tree of Life, we learn to consciously bridge our normal waking consciousness with the more subtle realms and temples of the subconscious mind. We learn to consciously awaken and manifest our most innate and forgotten abilities. Through the Tree, we develop more tangible links to subtle and ethereal realms, dimensions, beings and energies once thought beyond our reach. And we learn to access them whenever we desire to whatever degree we desire!

In the Tree of Life, our normal waking consciousness is represented by the level known as MALKUTH (the kingdom of Earth). It is the seat of all of the other energies of the universe. We are the microcosm. We have all of the divine energies of the universe within us. The difficulty is finding practical and effective ways of manifesting them consciously within our daily lives. The difficulty is bridging and linking our normal consciousness with those more subtle levels. This is where the Qabala truly shines.

Associated with each level of the Tree of Life are specific correspondences. These correspondences include divine names, symbols, sounds, colors, fragrances, magical images and more. They serve as doorbells to each corresponding level of our own subconscious mind, reflecting the energies and potentials inherent to within it. These energies and potentials become more available   to us and our life if we access these temples of the mind appropriately. This is what the Qabala teaches.

Every civilization and religion had its magical teachings. The phraseology may have differed and the symbols readapted, but only to conform to the needs of the time and the individuals. It is extraordinary though that there are so many similarities in methods used by magical traditions to change the consciousness of followers and practitioners. The Qabala encompasses most major magical traditions. It incorporates, numerology, tarot, mythology, astrology, mystical linguistics, healing sciences, and so regardless of one's personal magickal heritage, the Qabala will add even greater depth and power.

The basic correspondences in the Tree of Life were explored more fully in my predecessors to this volume. Later in this chapter, there are brief reviews of these basic correspondences. Throughout the rest of the book though, we will examine special techniques for using these correspondences to access and manifest our inner potentials more fully and more dynamically. That is when the magic of life begins to manifest!

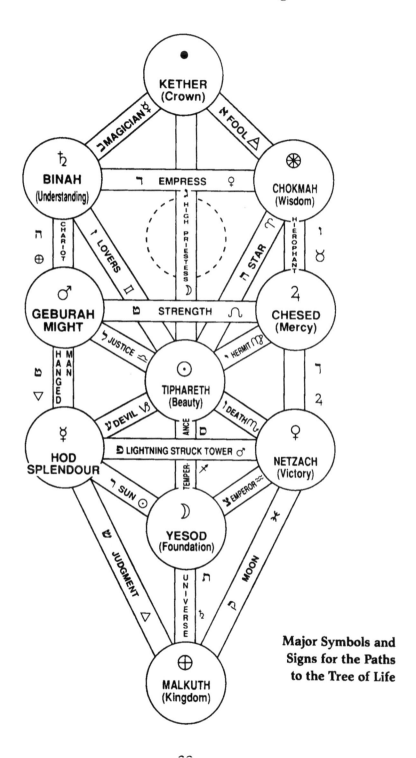

**Major Symbols and
Signs for the Paths
to the Tree of Life**

Tapping Archetypal forces

The process of using the Qabala to tap and release the magic within you begins with imbuing images and symbols with greater energy and strength to impact upon our conscious lives powerfully and effectively. It requires accessing and stimulating the primal core of their essence and then releasing and directing their force in a controlled manner into our daily lives. There are four distinct steps to this process:

1. Become conscious of the image reflecting a primal force/energy.

We must first become aware that every symbol and image that we use is a connection to and a reflection of a more primal, archetypal force. Carl Jung taught that all symbols and images could be placed in one of seven categories of archetypal forces within the universe. The closer we connect to an image's archetypal source, the greater the power we unleash. To accomplish a more primal connection, we must go beyond our usual logic in working with them. We must draw increasingly deeper associations and conclusions about the energies activated by the symbol or image that we use.

In the beginning we reflect upon the outer surface or most obvious significance and associations of the image. Even the most superficial focus upon an image or symbol will release some energy into your life from its archetypal source. As we continue to work with it, such as through the techniques in this book, we delve deeper into the cosmic spiral of its archetypal origins, and with each use of the symbol or image, we release more of its primal archetypal force into our outer physical world and daily life.

2. Immerse yourself deeply into the energy of the symbol or image.

The immersion into the image or symbol is sometimes called the magical action. It involves techniques that bring to the surface more of the archetypal energy hidden behind and operating through the image. This can be done through meditations, creative visualization and even through specific physical activities. It involves using techniques - such as pathworking - to adopt and absorb the energy of the image as our own. We learn to release it into our lives.

We then absorb and manifest the forces reflected by the images into our own individual essence. The various meditations and pathworking techniques will help you to link and merge your essence with the essence of the image's archetypal force. This is when we begin to create the magical body; we begin to manifest our most ideal potentials and essence.

To facilitate our merging with the archetypal forces, it is important to use some of the same symbols and images with all aspects of the Tree of Life. Each time we use them, we strengthen our connection to them and their archetypes. It enables us to get beyond surface levels of energies. For this reason, every time you enter one of the ten temples or a pathworking scenario, do so in the same manner.

3. Ground or earth the energy into your physical, waking and conscious life.

The grounding of the energy accessed is most critical to creating the magical life. This more than anything else is what distinguishes the effective techniques described in this book from fanciful imaginings, illusions, dreams and impotent creative visualizations and meditations that so many people complain about in the metaphysical field. All techniques may touch similar archetypal energies, but unless they are grounded, taken out of that ethereal mental realm, they will never work efficiently nor powerfully.

We are spiritual beings, but we live within a physical body and physical world. Those more ethereal, spiritual and archetypal forces we are accessing, must be earthed or grounded if they are to benefit us. If some tangible, physical activity is not used to ground the energies - to draw them out of the more subtle realms so they can express themselves more dynamically within our physical lives - they can create problems and imbalances.

Inappropriately grounded energies can often be identified by the following symptoms. They can stimulate nervousness, hypersensitivity, emotional outbursts, inability to sleep, a general sense of uneasiness, malaise, and other feelings of mental and emotional discomfort. Occasionally a sense of disruption and chaotic energies may also surface. If after a day or two of performing the exercises in this book you are experiencing several of these symptoms, you will need to ground yourself again. *Energy that is not grounded properly will find its own outlet - usually a disruptive one.*

On the other hand proper immersion and grounding of the energies will generate new awareness, insights, inspirations and creativity. There are, of course, the specific benefits and gifts that we attain through each temple and pathworking which are described later in the book. There are though more general responses that we will experience from properly accessing and grounding those archetypal energies.

Dream activity will become more vibrant and lucid. Physical energy will increase. Health will improve, and one of the more commonly experienced effects is that of increased sexual energy. Our sexual energy is a physical reflection of our creative life force. When we immerse ourselves more deeply into archetypal forces, our creative energies grow tremendously. The increased sexual energy is a tangible confirmation that the exercise worked, that the archetype was accessed - that the creative energy is flowing into your life.

The grounding begins with contemplation of the exercise, especially in the week following it. What have we experienced on all levels of our being since that time? What activities and events have unfolded since our performance of the exercise? Keeping a journal at least through one entire working of the Tree of Life is most essential to gaining the insight.

The performance of a physical action - even with something as simple as a journal - grounds the energy we have accessed into our physical lives. (Later we will learn more powerful - and yet simple - ways of accessing and grounding energy into our daily lives.) Grounding allows energy to express itself in a more balanced fashion. The contemplation and reflection upon the exercise and what has unfolded in our life since we performed the exercise is personal. It should be kept private and shared only with those who can truly help you to understand, i.e. a study group or a teacher. Sharing the experiences with others can dissipate the accessed energy, or through the responses of others may create blocks for the future. Comparing your responses to others will also create barriers.

4. Assimilate and evaluate the experience.

When we immerse ourselves in the images and symbols (step two) through the various exercises within this book, they will elicit responses within ourselves and within our lives - usually in a noticeable manner within 24-48 hours. Events that unfold in that time frame have often been triggered or brought to the forefront by your work with the symbols. Your work enables them to manifest more intensely.

After the immersion and grounding of the energy, there must be time to contemplate and assimilate the experience and its teaching. We must discern, examine and understand the intensity to our internal responses (physically, emotionally, mentally and spiritually). We must also monitor external effects as well by observing and noting what ensues in our daily life following the various exercises. This is the importance of the journal.

We must assess both our inner reactions and the outer effects. It is this monitoring and assessment that ultimately enables us to develop control and to open newer and greater forces. This may take a day, a week, a month or even longer - depending upon the individual, the method used, the symbol or images employed, and the circumstance in your life at the time.

When we use this process, we are learning to control and direct what we set in motion within our lives. We want to release energy to play out as intensely or as gently as we desire. When we can do this, we are living a magical life. Problems are resolved more easily. Tasks are accomplished more smoothly. Opportunities arise more frequently. People may see us as living a charmed existence, when in reality we are just working with the natural laws of the universe. It is this monitoring and seeing what actually unfolds within our lives following our exercises that provide the key to what seems to others as a magical control of life.

Developing the control is in part a trial and error process. If events that follow in our life are too intense or chaotic, then we know that next time we should change the manner in which we worked with the images. We can soften our focus and thus soften the impact within our life. In this way we learn to temper what we set in motion. This is what we will teach later in the book.

Yes, we know that certain images and symbols will generate certain kinds of effects within our life, but through the Qabala, we learn to generate the effects with great force or great gentleness. It is the assimilation, the post grounding process that enables us to understand the archetypal force and to delve only as deeply into it as we need each time.

Simple Guide for
Entering the Temples of the Mind.

1. Visulaize yourself entering into an ancient tree. You are encloaked in darkeness.

2. Speak the Divine name for the temple three times. With each repetition, imagine the temple becoming brighter and becoming the color associated with the temple.

3. In the temple is a stone altar. There is also a statue of the magical image associated with this temple. Laying upon or in front of the altar are the magical gifts of this Sephira.

4. Visualize a light begining to appear from behind the altar. From that light steps the archangel of the Sephira. The angel nods to you and extends arms to the side. There is a rumbling and rising from the floor - on either side of the altar come to pillars. One is white crystal and the other is black ebony. These are the pillars of balance.

5. To your amazement the statue of the magical image comes to life and presents you with the gifts of this temple. It then shimmers and melts into you. It becomes a growing part of you, to bless your life.

6. You give thanks for the gifts and the archangel steps forward and blesses you. The angel then fades back into the light behind the altar.

7. You slowly speak the divine names once more and the temple begins to dissolve around you.

8. You step out of the tree, bringing the gifts from the inner temple tou your outer life.

Aids to Bridging

The bridging and grounding of the archetypal energies to our physical life should at the very least involve the following. These physical activities are essential to experiencing the most powerful and beneficial effects of the exercises:

- Begin and end all exercises with a physical activity.

Use a vocal prayer, a posture or series of movements to reflect the opening and closing. Performing the "Balancing Pillars" described in part four will help, or you can create your own. Physical movement creates electrical changes in the body that help make us more receptive to the energies. They will amplify and facilitate your ability to access the archetypal energies, and they will help you also to ground them so that they manifest and work for you in a more balanced manner.

- Act out the lesson/experience of all temple visits and pathworkings.

Act out or pantomime the lesson or experience of the pathworking or temple visit. If you are trying to release energy that will bring more choice into your life, this might involve choosing to involve yourself in some new activity or endeavor within your life within 24 hours of the exercise. It is a physical way of sending a strong message to the universe that you will use all energy that you have activated. It also sends a message to the subconscious that you intend to utilize and act upon any energy that is released to you. The subconscious then feels free to access and release the archetypal energy into your life in great abundance.

and Grounding

- Keep a Tree of Life journal.

This doesn't have to be complicated or time consuming. Keep track of the date of the exercise, your feelings at the end of it and what occurs in your daily life over the next 48-72 hours or even a week. If you follow my suggestion of only performing one temple visit/ pathworking per week, it will be easier to discern how the energies are manifesting and playing out within your daily life. In part three are guidelines for creating and using a path working journal

Just the physical act of writing about the exercise and then keeping track of the major events that unfold will serve several functions. First it helps you to understand what you set it motion and how it is likely to play out within your life each time you do the same exercise. More importantly, it is a physical activity which helps ground the energy, helping you to handle it in a more balanced fashion.

- At the end of each exercise, eat something.

It doesn't have to be a full course meal. Eat something light. A few crackers will often suffice to help you feel more grounded and less flighty and disconnected.

- Stretch and perform some light physical work.

Again, it is a physical action that allows the energy to become earthed into your life, but in a more balanced fashion. If you feel disconnected and experience some of the symptoms mentioned earlier, perform some more vigorous physical activity. It will help to dissipate the disorienting effects.

Malkuth

WHAT CAN BE ATTAINED THROUGH THIS TEMPLE OF THE MIND:
Greater ability to discriminate in life; overcoming of inertia; insight for all problems of physical health (self or others) and into all affairs of the home; greater self-discovery; contact with elemental life forms and beings of Nature; at deepest level, vision of Holy Guardian Angel; discovery of things hidden within the physical universe; prosperity & security.

Symbolized by the Magical Images & Gifts of:
baskets of grain, sacred oils, jewels & gems of the Earth

DIVINE FORCE AVAILABLE: Adonai Ha-Aretz - Lord of the Earth
(Most direct influence over physical/material affairs)

ARCHANGEL MOST ACCESSIBLE: Sandalphon - Angel of Prayer and Life
(Answers prayers; formation of life; intercedes w/Holy Spirit)

SPIRITS MOST ACCESSIBLE: Ashim - Blessed Souls
(Saints & angels assisting Sandalphon)

TOOLS & IMAGES TO HELP ACCESS THIS LEVEL OF THE MIND:

Colors:	Black, olive, russet and citrine
Fragrance:	Sandalwood, lemon, carnation
Meditation Stones:	Smoky Quartz
Astrology:	Earth
Magical Image of You:	Young maiden, crowned and throned

WEAKNESSES THAT HINDER MANIFESTING POTENTIALS:
laziness, greed, avarice, over- reactive, aggressive, recklessness

STRENGTHS THAT ASSIST MANIFESTING POTENTIALS:
discrimination, prosperity, common   sense, physical energy, discernment

Yesod

WHAT CAN BE ATTAINED THROUGH THIS TEMPLE OF THE MIND:

Perception of rhythms of change; increased intuition & psychic abilities; dream consciousness; astral projection; true work with omens; strengthen emotional health; overcoming of idleness; at the deepest level, vision of the machinery of the universe (recognition of a divine plan at work).

Symbolized by the Magical Images & Gifts of:
silver winged slippers; mirror

DIVINE FORCE AVAILABLE: Shaddai El Chai -
Almighty Living God
(Aspect of divine recognized in all things)

ARCHANGEL MOST ACCESSIBLE: Gabriel -
Angel of Truth
(Guards gateways to other realms, instills hopes)

SPIRITS MOST ACCESSIBLE: Cherubim -
Beings of Light & Glory
(Keepers of celestial records)

TOOLS & IMAGES TO HELP ACCESS THIS LEVEL OF THE MIND:

Colors:	Violet; indigo
Fragrance:	Lavender, honeysuckle
Meditation Stones:	Amethyst
Astrology:	Moon
Magical Image of You:	Beautiful naked, strong man

WEAKNESSES THAT HINDER MANIFESTING POTENTIALS:
idleness; vanity; obsessive sex; impulsiveness; always a follower

STRENGTHS THAT ASSIST MANIFESTING POTENTIALS:
independence; spontaneity; dream study; conscious psychic development; self-awareness

Hod

WHAT CAN BE ATTAINED THROUGH THIS TEMPLE OF THE MIND:
Vision of truth; revelations of falsehood & deception; greater communication; knowledge of healing and magic; greater prosperity through increased knowledge; enhances any educational/scientific endeavor; at deepest level, a vision of the truth of our lives and truth in our lives.

Symbolized by the Magical Images & Gifts of:
Caduceus and staff

DIVINE FORCE AVAILABLE: Elohim Tzabaoth-
God of Wisdom & Harmony
(Divine overseeing of science, knowledge, evolution)

ARCHANGEL MOST ACCESSIBLE: Michael -
Angel of Balance, Protection
(Brings patience, protects against psychic dangers)

SPIRITS MOST ACCESSIBLE: Beni Elohim -
Divine Sons and Daughters
(Transmit divine consciousness & desire for the divine)

TOOLS & IMAGES TO HELP ACCESS THIS LEVEL OF THE MIND:

Colors:	Orange and peach
Fragrance:	Rosemary, frangipani, wisteria
Meditation Stones:	Citrine
Astrology:	Mercury
Magical Image of You:	Hermaphrodite

WEAKNESSES THAT HINDER HOD'S POTENTIALS:
deceit; impatience; dogmatism; over criticalness; separatism

STRENGTHS THAT ASSIST HOD'S POTENTIALS:
patience; practicality; knowledge; communication efforts; truthfulness

Netzach

WHAT CAN BE ATTAINED THROUGH THIS TEMPLE OF THE MIND:
Understanding of all relationships - especially love, unselfishness, artistic & creative inspiration, awakened sexuality, contact with Nature spirits (fairies & elves), awakened love and idealism, at the deepest level, a vision of our true beauty and that within others.

Symbolized by the Magical Images & Gifts of:
rose; wild flowers, sea shells

DIVINE FORCE AVAILABLE: Jehovah Tzabaoth -
God of Hosts
(Divine assistance with proper expression of emotions)

ARCHANGEL MOST ACCESSIBLE: Haniel -
Angel of Love and harmony
(Assists in artistic/creative endeavors)

SPIRITS MOST ACCESSIBLE: Elohim-
Gods and Goddesses (of all traditions)
(Protectors of religion, beliefs; inspire right decisions)

TOOLS & IMAGES TO HELP ACCESS THIS LEVEL OF THE MIND:

Color:	Emerald and all greens
Fragrance:	Patchouli, rose, bayberry
Meditation Stones:	Malachite; emerald
Astrology:	Venus
Magical Image of You:	Beautiful, sensual, naked woman

WEAKNESSES THAT HINDER NETZACH'S POTENTIALS:
emotionalism; worry; envy; lust; impurity; possessiveness

STRENGTHS THAT ASSIST NETZACH'S POTENTIALS:
warmth; optimism; time in nature; creative activities; expressiveness

Tiphareth

WHAT CAN BE ATTAINED THROUGH THIS TEMPLE OF THE MIND:

Greater and higher sense of devotion; Christ consciousness; glory and fame; more energy for life and success; harmony to things of the heart; victory over adversity; access to the true energy of the rainbow; healing on all levels; miracles: at the deepest level, awakens vision of rewards of devotion to Great Work (the achieving of the Holy Grail).

Symbolized by the Magical Images & Gifts of:
crown that is too large

DIVINE FORCE AVAILABLE: Jehovah Aloah Va Daath - God of Knowledge
(Divine aspect that creates through the power of mind)

ARCHANGEL MOST ACCESSIBLE: Raphael - Angel of Brightness & Healing
(Ministers all healing energies, healer of the divine)

SPIRITS MOST ACCESSIBLE: Malachim - Virtues or Angelic Kings
(Bestow grace; guardian angels; workers of miracles)

TOOLS & IMAGES TO HELP ACCESS THIS LEVEL OF THE MIND:

Colors:	Golden yellows; pink
Fragrance:	Rose; jasmine; lily
Meditation Stones:	Rose quartz
Astrology:	Sun
Magical Image of You:	Majestic king; the child; a sacrificed god

WEAKNESSES THAT HINDER TIPHARETH'S POTENTIALS:
false pride; self doubt; insecurity; irreverence; blaming

STRENGTHS THAT ASSIST TIPHARETH'S POTENTIALS:
reverence; idealism; nurturing; compassion; devotion

Geburah

WHAT CAN BE ATTAINED THROUGH THIS TEMPLE OF THE MIND:

Vision of natural forces and how to use; overcoming cruelty and destruction; greater strength & courage; energy for tearing down old & building the new; critical judgment; insight into enemies and discord; at the deepest level, awakens vision of one's true strength & courage and how to manifest it.

Symbolized by the Magical Images & Gifts of:
sword, spear, armor, weapons

DIVINE FORCE AVAILABLE: Elohim Gibor - God Almighty
(Divine aspect that protects; eliminates old for new growth)

ARCHANGEL MOST ACCESSIBLE: Kamael - Angel of Strength & Courage
(Defends/protects the weak & wronged; fights dragons)

SPIRITS MOST ACCESSIBLE: Seraphim - The Flaming Ones
(Assist in stopping those who upset our lives)

TOOLS & IMAGES TO HELP ACCESS THIS LEVEL OF THE MIND:

Color:	Reds; Fire shades
Fragrance:	Cinnamon; tobacco; gardenia; cypress
Meditation Stone:	Garnet
Astrology:	Mars
Magical Image of You:	Mighty warrior; warrior in a chariot

WEAKNESSES THAT HINDER GEBURAH'S POTENTIALS:
anger; fear; cruelty; self doubt; manipulation; belligerence

STRENGTHS THAT ASSIST GEBURAH'S POTENTIALS:
confidence; critical judgment; initiative; activity; dealing with issues

Chesed

WHAT CAN BE ATTAINED THROUGH THIS TEMPLE OF THE MIND:

Increased abundance; opportunities for prosperity; justice to one's life; hearing and recognizing the inner spiritual call; awakens greater peace and mercy; new growth and movement; at the deepest level, awakens a vision of love and true power at its most spiritual level.

Symbolized by the Magical Images & Gifts of:
cornucopia of treasures, king's cup

DIVINE FORCE AVAILABLE: El -
Divine, Mighty One
(Divine which reveals abundance, glory & grace of life)

ARCHANGEL MOST ACCESSIBLE: Tzadkiel -
Angel of Mercy
(Protects teachers; guardian of east winds of manifestation)

SPIRITS MOST ACCESSIBLE: Chasmalim -
Brilliant Ones
(Dominations; manifest / awaken majesty in our life)

TOOLS & IMAGES TO HELP ACCESS THIS LEVEL OF THE MIND:

Colors:	Blues; purples
Fragrances:	Bayberry; cedar; nutmeg
Meditation Stones:	Lapis Lazuli
Astrology:	Jupiter
Magical Image of You:	Mighty, crowned & throned ruler (king/queen)

WEAKNESSES THAT HINDER CHESED'S POTENTIALS:
hypocrisy; dogmatism; smugness; self-righteousness; false pride; bigotry

STRENGTHS THAT ASSIST CHESED'S POTENTIALS:
idealism; truth & loyalty; patience; devotion; endurance; committedness

Binah

WHAT CAN BE ATTAINED THROUGH THIS TEMPLE OF THE MIND:
Understanding & meaning of sorrows, sacrifices and burdens; all mother-type information; deeper relationship with Mother Nature; new birth; uncovering of secrets; at its deepest level, it awakens a vision of and understanding for the processes of birth and death.
Symbolized by the Magical Images & Gifts of:
robe of many colors, cloak of concealment, yoni

DIVINE FORCE AVAILABLE:
Jehovah Elohim -
Perfection of Creation
(Divine aspect that gives understanding & new birth)

ARCHANGEL MOST ACCESSIBLE:
Tzaphkiel -
Angel of Spiritual Strife against Evil
(brings understanding; eases sorrows; aids rebirth)

SPIRITS MOST ACCESSIBLE:
Aralim -
Strong and Mighty Ones
(Give sustenance & understanding; guard Mother Earth)

TOOLS & IMAGES TO HELP ACCESS THIS LEVEL OF THE MIND:

Colors:	Black; all colors
Fragrances:	Eucalyptus; myrrh; chamomile; sage
Meditation Stones:	Obsidian; black tourmaline
Astrology:	Saturn
Magical Image of You:	Mature woman; matron; crone

WEAKNESSES THAT HINDER BINAH'S POTENTIALS:
impatience; greed; fear of future; unnecessary martyrdom; lack of confidentiality

STRENGTHS THAT ASSIST BINAH'S POTENTIALS:
patience; silence; faithfulness; nurturing; discipline; strength of will

Chokmah

WHAT CAN BE ATTAINED THROUGH THIS TEMPLE OF THE MIND:

Greater initiative; opportunities for new undertakings; pure source of life-giving energy; any father-type information; realization of hidden abilities; revelations of things concealed; understanding of astrology and the influence of the stars; at its deepest level, it awakens a vision of the divine, face to face.

Symbolized by the Magical Images & Gifts of:
Scepter of power, staff, phallus

DIVINE FORCE AVAILABLE: Jah (Jehovah) -
Divine, Ideal Wisdom
(Divine that oversees the heavens influence upon us)

ARCHANGEL MOST ACCESSIBLE: Ratziel -
Angel of Hidden Knowledge & Concealment
(Teaches & reveals starry and hidden influences)

SPIRITS MOST ACCESSIBLE: Auphanim -
Whirling Forces
(Assist in visions of spiritual forces)

TOOLS & IMAGES TO HELP ACCESS THIS LEVEL OF THE MIND:

Colors:	Grays; fog & smoke tones
Fragrances:	Eucalyptus; musk; geranium
Meditation Stones:	Fluorite
Astrology:	Neptune
Magical Image of You:	Older, bearded male figure

WEAKNESSES THAT HINDER CHOKMAH'S POTENTIALS:
inefficiency; procrastination; envy; superstitious; fear of the future

STRENGTHS THAT ASSIST CHOKMAH'S POTENTIALS:
initiative; devotion; study of stars; goal oriented; idealism

Kether

WHAT CAN BE ATTAINED THROUGH THIS TEMPLE OF THE MIND:
Creativity and artistic inspiration; revelations of endings and beginnings; opportunities and energies for change and transition; new insight into spiritual path; intensifying of any aspect of life or evolutionary path; Initiation of new life and opportunities; reveals what must be done to complete life's work and how to do it.
Symbolized by the Magical Images & Gifts of:
spinning top; spark of light; tinder box

DIVINE FORCE AVAILABLE: Eheieh -
I Am That I Am
(Deepest spiritual aspect of divine we can experience)

ARCHANGEL MOST ACCESSIBLE: Metatron -
King of Angels
(Links divine and humans; gifted human with Qabala)

SPIRITS MOST ACCESSIBLE: Chaioth ha-Qadesh -
Holy Living Creatures
(Reveal love, light & fire in humans & nature)

TOOLS & IMAGES TO HELP ACCESS THIS LEVEL OF THE MIND:

Colors:	Brilliant white
Fragrances:	Frankincense; ambergris; sage
Meditation Stones:	Double terminated quartz; Herkimer diamond
Astrology:	Uranus
Magical Image of You:	Ancient, bearded king (seen only in profile)

WEAKNESSES THAT HINDER KETHER'S POTENTIALS:
excessive daydreaming; shame; self denial; unsympathetic; poor self image

STRENGTHS THAT ASSIST KETHER'S POTENTIALS:
creative imagination; sense of wonder; embrace change; order

Chapter Three

Masks of the Sephiroth

Masks have always had a magical power about them. Concealed behind it, we can become something or somebody else. We can become whatever we want to be by wearing a mask. Whether a simple headdress or helmet mask, it helped to enlarge you. To own a mask is to possess a potential power. The wearer magically assumes a new identity. It enables present reality to be suspended.

Masks are invested with mystery. They are tools for transformation. They are equivalent to the process of chrysalis. Metamorphosis usually is and should be hidden, so it is not interrupted. The hidden aspect, the secrecy, leads to transfiguration. It helps us to change what we are to what we want to be, giving us magic.

There is an ambiguity and an equivocation about masks. The ambiguity is the fact that when we wear one, we are no longer whom we thought. The equivocation is that we are making ourselves one with some other force. By wearing a mask, we become part of the mythical "'Tween Times and Places". We move into an intersection between the outer real world and other dimensions. We create a doorway of the mind - a threshold that we can cross to new dimensions and beingness. When working with masks of the Tree of Life, we move into a more intimate link with universal forces outside of us and those sleeping within us. We are less passive and more active, bringing the energies and magic of the Qabala alive more strongly.

Mystery of Mask Making

The origin of masks is unclear, although there is very ancient evidence of their use all over the world. This evidence has been found in artifacts and in literature. Mask making is an ancient art employed all over the world for ceremony, celebration and in magical practices. The Tibetans wore masks to represent ghouls and skeletons in devil dances at the seasons of the year. The Chinese used papier-mache masks in religious drama. On Java, people used masks of wood in celebrations and ceremonies, often supplemented with shadow puppet presentations. The Suka males of the Congo during ceremonial dances following circumcision rituals wore helmet masks. The Aztecs used mosaic masks for worship and celebration.

The Greeks in their amphitheater wore large masks so the audience at a distance could see them. They were constructed with a tube to amplify the voice. The miracle and mystery plays of the early church often involved the priest wearing masks to represent metaphorical ideas such as death, the devil and life itself. The Noh plays of Japan - also developed in the 14th century - were highly stylized, each movement and each speech done precisely as it has always been done before. Today about 250 of them still exist. Men play all of the roles, using at least 125 kinds of full face masks made of lacquered wood.

In Italy, full face, half-face and masks with beaks became an art form during the Renaissance. Mummers in Great Britain and in colonial America were masked actors who around Christmas time portrayed characters such as Father Christmas.

To the North American native peoples spirits influence all aspects of life and are found in all things. To the Inuit of the Bering Sea even gnarled driftwood has an "Inua", a dwelling force that gives it meaning, real existence and life. Such pieces of wood were often carved into masks or made a part of a mask. Different Native American societies had their own mask making techniques and rituals. The Iroquois had their twisted facemasks. The Pueblo have their Kachina masks, and the Inuit their wooden masks.

Probably the most famous is the Iroquois False Face Society. The Iroquois nation was comprised of six tribes: the Mohawk, the Oneida, the Onondaga, the Cyuga, the Seneca, and the Tuscarora. They held the belief that all disease was caused by evil spirits, and at such a time, help would be asked of the False Face Society.

One could only become a member of the society if you had been cured by it. It was comprised of mostly men, and there had to have been a dream of becoming a member. That dream had to be confirmed by another member. In the dream, the dream spirit instructs the individual how to make a healing mask and gives the individual his own healing song.

In Africa and America alike, most masks were considered the property of the secret societies, and only the members were allowed to wear them. When they were not in use, they were always kept covered. And no two masks were ever alike. Often men were only allowed to wear the masks, but women also had their secret societies, possessing their own masks. Every mask was individual, and each had its own story.

Purposes of Masks

1. Worn ceremonially to appease certain forces,
2. Worn to communicate with the spirits and the supernatural,
3. Worn to scare children and give them warnings,
4. Worn to terrorize the enemy,
5. Worn to teach through storytelling,
6. Worn to represent mythological being or creature,
7. Worn as a memorial,
8. Worn to connect with animals or some other force in nature,
9. Work to make rain or control the elements,
10. Worn to prevent illness and cure disease,
11. Worn for drama and theater,
12. Worn to facilitate shapeshifting,
13. Worn to court a lover,
14. Worn for amusement,
15. Worn as ornamentation,
16. Worn for ritual and initiation
17. Worn to facilitate change of consciousness,
18. Worn for fertility and sexuality,
19. Worn to represent family and clans,
20. Others

Masks of the Sephiroth

If we wish to empower the process of tapping our innermost powers and potentials, reflected by the Tree of Life, we can use simple ritualistic techniques. These can be formal or informal. The most effective and simplest is the use of some kind of costuming and body art. Appropriate costuming and body art can align us with and invoke the archetypal energies represented by the Tree of Life. For example, we can put on body art – designs and colors associated with a Sephira, and we immediately begin to align with that temple. Resonance begins to be established. It triggers a response in a corresponding part of the subconscious mind.

There are many kinds of body art that can be used to enhance Qabalistic rituals, ceremonies and exercises. And it can be as simple as wearing clothing that is the color associated with the temple or by painting the Hebrew letters and other symbols of that temple upon our body. It can also include tattooing, body paint, costuming, and jewelry. They are all effective in helping us establish a connection with and manifesting the energies of each level of the tree of life. And this in turn, helps us access the level of our mind where these powers are often lying dormant. The more of these aids that we use, the stronger the associated level of our mind is stimulated, opening access to greater potentials.

I do not recommend tattooing, but the body can be decorated less permanently to enhance the significance of Qabalistic work. Many societies incorporated body painting as part of their rituals. The face, hands and other parts of the body can be marked with signs, images and colors that reflect the Sephira and our purpose for tapping the Tree of Life. Henna / Mehndi body art is one of the newest ways and can be very powerful. There are also many face-painting kits on the market today. Many are hypo-allergenic and are easily washed off with soap and water.

In this way, you can adjust more easily the body markings to your purpose.

Costumes and ceremonial dress have often been used in various ritual traditions. Simple robes can be made in the appropriate colors of the sephiroth. I have found that simple is often better. In my work with the Tree of Life over the years, I have accumulated sweatshirts in the basic colors of the sephiroth. If I intend to be working on a particular level, I simply pull out the proper sweatshirt. If you are more industrious, there are many clothing paints available that are inexpensive. Tree of Life Symbols, Hebrew letters and astrological symbols can be added to reinforce your connection. The simple process of decorating a robe or even a sweatshirt begins the process of ringing the doorbell of the corresponding level of your subconscious mind. The putting on of the costume initiates a mental shift so that we begin to align on the energy of sephira. Another aspect of costuming that can be used to connect to the animal in your shapeshifting rites is through related jewelry. The more of the temple's elements that you include in your exercises, the stronger your alignment and resonance with the corresponding level of your mind.

Of all of the costuming aids, the most important and powerful is the simple mask. It is a tool that is one of the most effective for opening yourself to the true power of the Qabalistic Tree of Life and for manifesting our hidden potentials.

Making and Using Qabala Masks

Through the ages, ceremonial and meditation masks have been made from a variety of materials. These include, but are not limited to, fiber, wood, shell, bone, feathers, hides, cloth, bark, leaves and even husks. The materials and the making of the masks were done usually in solitude and with great deliberation and concentration on the force to be awakened by the mask. The mask making was never rushed. The twisted-face masks of the Iroquois were often carved into a tree and then cut out from the tree. It had to be done with deliberation and without harming the tree. Powerful masks associated with the Tree of Life do not have to be anywhere near as complicated as that.

Remember that masks are tools for transformation. As mentioned, they are equivalent to the process of chrysalis. Metamorphosis usually is hidden, so it is not interrupted. When we put on a mask associated with a sephira, we shift from the outer world and begin the journey of tapping the hidden inner aspects of us that we may have neglected or not even known about. The mask separates us from our normal consciousness and helps us move to a new awareness within ourselves. It leads to an awakening of that level of the mind and an awakening of its inherent potentials and powers - ultimately leading to a transfiguration of ourselves. In essence, it changes our perception of what we are to what we want to be, freeing our magic.

When we put on a mask of a sephira, we are no longer whom we thought. We make ourselves one with some other force. In this case, it is the magical force associated with one of the Temples on the Tree of Life – a magical force lying dormant within us. By wearing a sephiroth mask, we move between the outer real worlds into new dimensions. We create a shifting of the mind and a threshold that we can cross to new dimensions and beingness. We are less passive and more active, bringing the energy of the Tree of Life alive more strongly within us and our life.

Keep the making of sephiroth masks simple. I recommend starting with simple plastic mask forms that can be found at any hobby shop. They are inexpensive and you can purchase ten – one for each of the sephiroth on the Tree of Life. Paint the mask the color of the sephira that you will be tapping. You can also add other symbols, Hebrew letters and such that correspond to that sephira to enhance the power of the mask.

In the example below, I show a simple version of a Binah mask that I made many years ago and still use. The mask is painted black, the primary color for Binah. I also painted on it the Hebrew letters for the Divine name associated with it and I painted the astrological symbol of Saturn. Underneath one of the eyes, I painted three tears. Binah is the third sephira on the Tree of Life and one of the magical images is the sorrowful mother filled with understanding. In the area of the third eye, there is a small crystal to facilitate inner vision and understanding. This is a mask that I often use when I work with Binah to open deeper perception and understanding of hidden things going on around me.

Later when we learn to do more powerful techniques of pathworking, you can take one of these masks forms and paint each side of the face with the color and symbols of the two sephiroth that you are linking through the pathworking process.

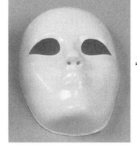

Simple plastic mask form

Mask for Binah

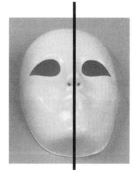

For pathworking mask, divide it in half and decorate one half for one Sephira and one half for the other.

Creating a Sephira Mask

The process of making a Sephira mask is very simple. *Know what force you wish your mask to represent.* Review the sephira and its attributes and associations. Know that the more significance you can find in it, the greater ability it will have to help you make the transformations you wish.

Mask making does not need to be a complicated affair. Begin with simple masks, so that you can experience the enjoyment of the creative process and be freer to feel the energies awakened by the mask. I like to use the plastic mask forms that can be found at most hobby shops. They are easily painted. They easily hold the form for papier mache and even wet plaster if you wish to make more intricate masks.

Paint the mask with the symbols and colors of the Sephiroth. In time though you may wish to become more elaborate in how the masks reflect the power of that particular temple. Subtlety has its place in the beginning but as you grow with the Tree and the Tree grows within you, something more elaborate may be suitable. Most ritual masks have exaggerated qualities about them. It helps the individual to make the shift in consciousness to that which is greater than the self.

Don't rush the process or compare it to others. What you do with your mask will be most effective for you. Take your time, and keep in mind that with each part of the process - when done with deliberation - you empower the mask to help you begin to transform yourself, making you more receptive to manifesting the energy and power of the Sephira.

Make your mask as comfortable as you can. Remember that a mask needs air holes you can breathe. Although some traditions utilized a "bondage" or sensory- deprivation mask for specific initiation purposes, these were only employed under the strictest conditions because of their ability to augment radical changes in consciousness.

Use ordinary and simple materials in making and decorating your masks. Keep in mind though that as you do, you are using the ordinary for extraordinary purposes. It is a reminder that no matter how ordinary or inconsequential we may feel our life to be we can still manifest the extraordinary within it. Use beads, dried flowers, feathers, lace, paints, rhinestones, ribbons and whatever you have available. Be as elaborate with the materials as you wish.

When you are not using your masks, keep them covered. It them more powerful, and the energies evoked by them are not allowed to leak or dissipate. It is a way of reverencing and honoring the forces of the mask. For temple masks, or those that are hung for decoration, this is not necessary. Temple masks are often reminders to us of the forces within our life. If you choose to make the wall mask more powerful for you, you may wish to have candles next to it. The lighting of the candles can be visualized as the igniting and activating of the forces represented by the mask.

Use your imagination in the creation of the mask. Your designs and the forces you invoke through them are only limited by your own imagination. Remember that masks help us make transitions from our normal, ordinary levels of consciousness to those beyond. As you open and express your imagination through the creation of the masks, you expand the opportunities to connect with greater power and force. You move closer to the primal energy and essence that is you or part of you. Above all have fun with the process. Creation and imagination are necessary to enjoy ourselves fully.

9. Use ritual to help awaken the power of the mask.
Ritual dances help make lifeless masks animated. Ordinary ceremonies become dynamic spiritual dramas. Masks and movement empower each other. Ritual is a creative process and so should the making of costumes and the imbuing it with energy.

The making of a sephira mask is fun, but for the mask to be effective, it must be secure and comfortable and it should not restrict breathing, speech or sight. Later in this book you will learn how to perform simple but dynamic Qabala dances for tapping the sephiroth and for empowering pathworking. The use of your masks with these will make them even more effective – awakening your inherent magic in ways that will amaze you.

Awakening the Sephira's Power

1. Make sure you will not be disturbed.

2. Have your mask available. If you do not have a mask available, you can use body art, painting the face and body to reflect the sephira.

3. Know what your movements will be. (Refer to chapter 8.)

4. Have an opening and grounding posture. This helps prevent disorientation and that "spacey feeling". These will be explored later in the book.

5. Awaken the temple as you learned in the previous chapter by speaking the Divine name of the temple and then visualizing it taking form around you.

6. Now place the mask over your face. Then imagine, see and feel yourself transforming. Imagine the magickal image coming to life within the temple. See it before you and greet it.

7. See the magical image shimmer and then melt into you. Feel yourself becoming the magical image with all of its inherent powers. Feel its energy and qualities coming alive stronger within you with every breath that you take. Visualize how you will be able to apply its qualities to your life.

8. Offer thanks to this aspect of the Divine for awakening within you and your life.

9. Perform your grounding posture and feel your self returning to your human essence, but strengthened by the magickal image that is now a part of you.

10. Close the temple as you learned in the previous chapter.

Part II -

The Secret
of
Daath

Chapter Four

The Secret
of Daath

In more ancient times mystical knowledge was hidden from the general public. Today, mystical and metaphysical knowledge is more available to the general public than ever before. There exist tremendous amounts of knowledge about all aspects of mysticism. This abundance of knowledge influences all levels of awareness and consciousness - even as it is reflected within the Tree of Life.

We have more knowledge today of the workings of life on Earth than at any other time in history. The mysteries of nature are being unveiled at an unprecedented rate. The once theoretical and invisible atom is today a scientific and physical reality. This is an example of knowledge influencing us through Malkuth or Earth.

We understand the psycho-structure of the human mind in ways never before comprehended. This is knowledge influencing us through the level of Yesod. Scientific realms are aligning with the alchemical teachings of the past. Science and magic are not as distant as once believed. This is knowledge influencing us and manifesting through the level of Hod. Meditation on the knowledge inherent within each sephira will yield great benefits to the spiritual student.

Knowledge of every aspect of the Tree of Life is more

available to the general public than ever before. Knowledge and its ability to stimulate and affect different levels of consciousness are more predominant than ever with an increased ability to accelerate the awakening of our sleeping potentials. This increased mystical knowledge is a reality, and it is only hidden in that it lies behind and influences all aspects of the Tree of Life.

If we wish to climb the Tree of Life and ascend to greater heights of awareness, we must have a disciplined inner schooling. Such schooling can enable us to attain knowledge of the divinely creative worlds and the beings that belong to them. Through careful preparation our inner potentials can be realized.

In the modern Qabala - in modern work with the Tree of Life - this is accomplished through the hidden sephira referred to as *DAATH*. Daath is not an original concept of the Qabala. In fact, early Qabalistic teachings speak of ten and only ten sephiroth or levels on the Tree of Life. Daath or Knowledge is only mentioned in conjunction with either Binah or Chokmah. Today we must view it as a separate level of consciousness in its own right.

Daath has been called the invisible level, hidden within the Great Abyss that separates the bottom seven levels from the three upper. As seen in the following diagram, it bridges the seven lower levels of consciousness to the three higher, more abstract levels.

It bridges the levels of consciousness that are easier for us to access to those which are more difficult to work with and control, and it is only hidden today in that it lies behind and influences all other levels of consciousness.

When we can bring the upper levels to play more dynamically within our lives, along with the lower seven, then we are truly living the Tree of Life. Through Daath this becomes more easily accomplished. Daath, or higher knowledge, becomes the bridge to heightened consciousness and higher initiation for the modern spiritual student. But that greater knowledge also entails *much greater responsibility.*

Daath Becoming Visible
on the Tree of Life

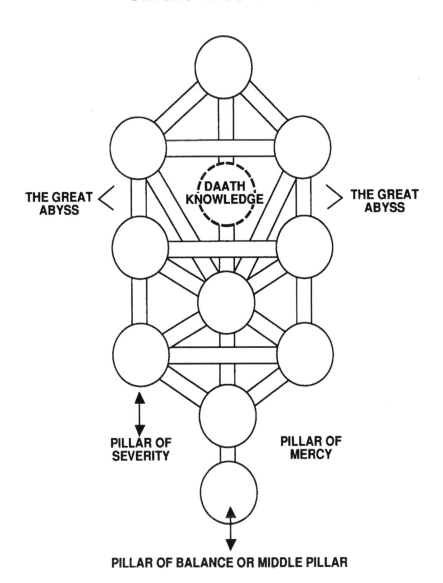

The Mystery of Daath

Daath is the eleventh sephira on the Tree of Life. It is the hidden temple of knowledge. Although absent from the earliest teaching of the Qabala, it has found itself increasingly part of Qabalistic lore over the more recent centuries. As mentioned, it is called the invisible sephira, hidden within the Great Abyss that separates the seven lower levels from the three upper.

It is significant that Daath falls within the area of the Tree of Life known as the Great Abyss. Knowledge brings to light many of the fears and superstitions that we hold. Knowledge serves to move us through the abyss of our darkest doubts and superstitions in every area of life. Knowledge sheds light upon the natural and supernatural worlds.

Many times in unfolding our spiritual energies, the heightened initiation we seek does not occur until we are able to tap more fully those levels of consciousness that serve to integrate the more pure, abstract energies of the universe. The levels of our consciousness that work with these abstract forces are what we call Binah, Chokmah and Kether in the Tree of Life.

We can manifest tremendous potentials from the other seven - often times more tangibly than the upper three, but until we link the upper three with the lower seven, even the lower levels will have limits of manifestation within our lives. This is what makes Daath so critical to our path of spiritual evolution.

Daath becomes the bridge between the lower seven and the upper three. It is what creates the true alchemical transmutation within us on a soul level. It is this crossing of the abyss through higher knowledge that is reflected in the Biblical story of Elijah who "saw God and was no more". He accessed the energies on the other side of the abyss, and it created a permanent change in consciousness and perception. The old no longer existed, for something new was created.

Daath or knowledge helps us to work from all levels of consciousness associated with the Tree of Life. As our knowledge of the energies available to us at each level grows, we are propelled more strongly along our own unique path in life. Universally, Daath operates and affects the awakening of all energies at all levels of our consciousness. The more we know about a particular level of consciousness, the more we can use it to benefit our lives.

It is because of Daath that we are able to work on each individual level and awaken their corresponding energies, thereby increasing our understanding (Binah) of our own purposes in life and increasing our wisdom (Chokmah) so that we may act upon that understanding. By doing so, we may touch the highest aspects of our own consciousness (Kether), linking us more solidly with the Divine.

Prior to fully tapping the level of Daath, the spiritual student is still in the process of becoming - still awakening to the various levels of consciousness and their energies. When we learn to unite Daath with the others, when knowledge operates fully and consciously with each of the other levels of consciousness, then we are capable of integrating present physical life with universal life. Then we enter true discipleship, and we are thereafter involved in the process of being rather than becoming. At this point the soul has access to all that was, is and will be. This does NOT mean though that the soul can employ it all, but it would have access to it.

There is great significance to Daath being placed upon the middle pillar of the Tree of Life. Knowledge can balance us, but knowledge misused will result in misplaced force and imbalance within our lives. The idea of "a little knowledge being a dangerous thing" is apropo here. Our fears and doubts, and even our inbred, societal superstitions - represented by the Great Abyss - can cause us to use our knowledge inappropriately. Daath on the middle pillar reminds us to balance information and knowledge with appropriate discrimination (Malkuth), independent testing and work (Yesod) and appropriate devotion (Tiphareth) if we are to touch the crown of our own divinity (Kether).

Daath in the Human Body

On a more personal level, within the human body Daath is associated with the throat chakra. This is our center of will and creative expression. The throat chakra is very important to the modern spiritual aspirant, for it contains a key to the secret of regeneration. Through it can be found the teachings for the magical power of sound and voice.

The Divine aspect associated with the heart of the Tree of Life (Tiphareth) and thus our own heart center is called *Jehovah Aloah va Daath* or "God made manifest in the sphere of the mind". In other words our thoughts are at the heart of what manifests within our lives. They create most of our life circumstances. When we give voice to those thoughts, appropriately or not, we draw their energies out of the ethereal mental realm and ground them, releasing them more dynamically into our physical lives. Yes, our thoughts affect us, but when we give them voice, their effects manifest more quickly and more clearly.

The creation and manifestation of our thoughts into our physical world is part of the power of Daath acting through the throat chakra. We are activating our own innate Daath consciousness, giving greater power to our thoughts. Remember that Daath is the link between the energies of the higher mind with the lower levels of consciousness. It is why the ancient masters strongly encouraged and practiced reticence of speech.

Daath, like all of the sephiroth, has specific energies associated with it and with its function in our lives. It has a Divine aspect that is most predominant, as well as archangelic and angelic beings that can be touched by tapping this level more fully. It is linked to specific energies in the physical universe as, with corresponding virtues and vices (unbalanced expressions of the energies tapped).

Daath in the Human Microcosm

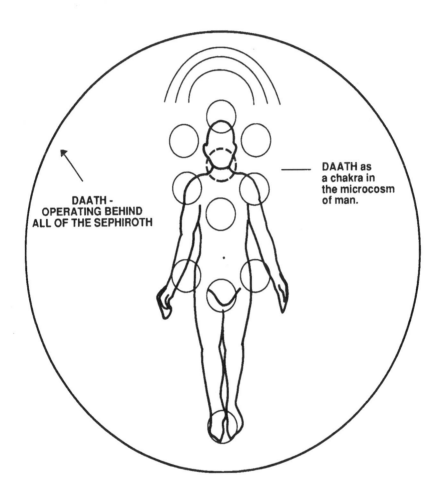

DAATH -
OPERATING BEHIND
ALL OF THE SEPHIROTH

DAATH as
a chakra in
the microcosm
of man.

Daath not only works to release knowledge of each level of consciousness, but also serves as a separate consciousness as well, wherein universal knowledge of all the spiritual and esoteric sciences can be attained. On a lesser level, it also corresponds to the throat chakra, the center of will and creative expression within humans. It is a center of cornucopia because through proper use and understanding of it, we can learn to manifest all we need from any of the other levels of consciousness.

The Power of Daath

That aspect of the Divine which can be experienced at this level of our consciousness is actually a combination of the Divine aspects associated with and experienced through Binah and Chokmah. The Divine name *Jehovah Elohim* is the name most appropriate for the Divine force accessible through Daath. This name can be interpreted as *the Divine which manifests the perfection of creation and the life of the world to come.* This fits Daath and Daath's function within our daily lives, for through knowledge, we can create a new life or a world to come.

Because of Daath's association with the throat chakra and thus the power of voice, we can use this Divine name with proper visualization to add tremendous power to all of our affirmations, mantras and other words of power. It literally empowers the throat chakra for greater manifestation. Toning the name prior to and just after our prayers and affirmations will make them ever more effective and powerful.

No single archangel was ever associated with the level of Daath. Usually, the archangels of the four cardinal points are assigned and more accessible through this level of our consciousness. Raphael is for the East, Michael is the South, Gabriel is the West and Auriel is for the North. This is appropriate because learning comes to us from all directions if we learn to recognize it. These magnificent beings can help us learn from all things within our world. Invoking their aid and guidance before any work on the level of Daath surrounds us with protection and helps us to use knowledge with fewer imbalances.

On the other hand, since all of the archangels serve as teachers for the different sephiroth, any archangel can work through Daath. Teachers disseminate knowledge, and Daath is the sphere of knowledge. Any teacher we work with - human or angelic - helps us to activate the Daath level of our own consciousness.

Working with the archangels is a group of spirits or

angelic beings similar to the seraphim. My own personal experience has been very similar. I have found them very serpent-like, casting a silver flame or light about them. Their eyes always appeared mistlike, shifting like the mist upon a lake in the early morning. I find this appropriate in that our knowledge is always shifting our perceptions into new waves and forms. With everyone though there will be some differences because these beings will interact with each person's energies in a unique manner.

On a more mundane level the energy available to us through Daath is astrologically comparable to Sirius, the Dog Star. In Egyptian mythology the name Sirius is traced to the god Osiris, and it was considered the resting place of the soul of Isis. In fact the Isis mythology can be used most easily in awakening the energies of Daath within ourselves.

Osiris and Isis are both attributed to Sirius and thus also to Daath. Isis is the supreme feminine (Binah) and Osiris is the supreme masculine (Chokmah). Their union occurs on the mundane level in Daath. The technique of using myths and tales to tap the various levels of our consciousness is is very powerful and is explored more fully in my book *More Simplified Magic*.

In astrology if Sirius is well placed, it denotes or can contribute to wealth, fame, honor, etc. within one's life. All of these are things which greater knowledge can lead to within our individual lives. The world is a world of abundance, an abundance that everyone can share in if we KNOW how. Through Daath we come to know. Not only does it reflect the union of Binah and Chocmah (the union of the female and the male from which comes new birth), but it also unites Geburah and Chesed, energy and abundance.

There are other aspects associated with Daath that can help us tap this level of consciousness. Candles of the appropriate colors and a corresponding fragrance can make our task more easily accomplished. The colors that reflect and which can be used are grays and lavenders - particularly the grays. Gray is like a cloud which hides knowledge behind it.

Some fragrances are also effective in creating an atmosphere that facilitates touching this level of consciousness. Lilac, bay oil and wisteria are three of the more effective for Daath. More generic fragrances, such as sandalwood or frankincense, can also be used.

Magical Symbols and Images of Daath

Learning to change our world creatively is what we attempt through the Qabala and the techniques of working with it. The symbols and images of Daath are vague at best because the energies they awaken are fluid and changeable. Each new bit of knowledge changes all that was previously learned. When we change our imaginings, we change our world. Through working specifically with Daath the images and symbols we use at all levels are empowered to become reality. Our dreams become more capable of manifesting. Daath gives the images and symbols life, stimulating the cosmic spiral on the middle pillar.

The magical image of Daath operates in many ways like the archangels - as a teacher. It is usually the image of a man with two faces, each looking in opposite directions. This is the mythical image of Janus. In Roman mythology Janus was the planter of seeds and the god of good beginnings, ruling the past and the future. He protected the health, happiness and material wealth of the family. Janus was the guardian of doors, gateways, bridges, entrances and exits. Janus was believed to open and close the gates of heaven. All of this reflects the power of Daath and the importance of knowledge in life.

The image of a face looking in opposite directions reminds us that unless knowledge is used correctly, it will result in either looking or using it only where we have already been. We must use it to move us beyond where we are, across the abyss to higher evolution. It is also a reminder that knowledge must always be balanced.

Magical Symbols & Images of Daath

Janus

The Crescent

The Pentagram

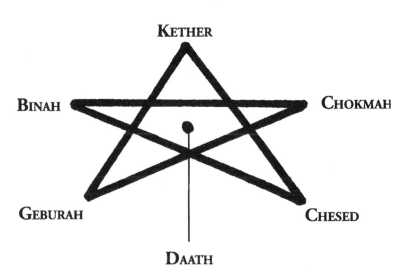

As you will discover, this image will help open your own vision across the abyss. Just as Janus opened the doors to heaven, Daath opens to us knowledge of the heavens and how to achieve it. This image helps to awaken a vision of the new life to come - a life which can bring hope, fulfillment and a heightened sense of will and destiny.

One of the other symbols associated with Daath is the pentagram. Daath is the heart of the pentagram, with the five points touching Kether, Binah, Chokmah, Geburah and Chesed. (See the diagram.) It links the lower sephiroth with the three supernals in the Tree of Life. It is a geometric shape which activates the higher energies of the individual so there is dominion of the spirit over the elements - reason over matter.

The pentagram, the five-pointed star, is an ancient sign of the microcosm. It is a symbol of humanity with arms and legs extended and the head touching the creator. At the heart of the microcosm is Daath - knowledge which helps us realize that all of the energies of the universe already exist within us.

The crescent is also a symbol for Daath. This moon symbol is more strongly related to Yesod, but Daath is a deeper level of Yesod. They both reflect energies of the subconscious, with Daath supplying the knowledge of how to use those energies more appropriately. Daath can be taken as the higher, more spiritual energies of Yesod.

The crescent is an ancient symbol. This geometric shape can be a link to the archetypal forces that enhance healing of emotional imbalances. It can be used to help with problems of expression. Both of these aspects relate it to Daath. Through greater self-knowledge we can face and transmute our lower emotions, freeing our own creative expressions.

The crescent also awakens the feminine energies of our soul - our intuitive, receptive aspects. We are all a combination of masculine and feminine expressions of energy. This is part of what the Qabala teaches. The feminine are the intuitive, illuminated and enlightened aspects of the soul, our birth giving energies. Knowledge, innate within us all, has the potential to illumine and enlighten. When it does, we begin to give birth to our higher self.

The crescent is a shape that is also connected to nada yoga, the dynamic and creative use of sounds and mantras. Again, this reflects the association of Daath with the throat chakra in the human body. It reinforces the influence of Daath as tied to our center of expression for creativity and manifestation.

Daath as the Sphere of Justice

Daath is located in the Abyss, the center of our deepest levels of subconscious fears and inner demons. Tapping Daath places us right in the midst of them, where we have little choice but to deal with them. It is for this reason that Daath is also known as *THE SPHERE OF JUSTICE*. True justice involves confronting and dealing with what must ultimately be faced.

Through Daath, we open to knowledge of all deeds - past, present and future. Through Daath, knowledge of things hidden is revealed and brought to full consciousness. This can be severely disruptive to the soul and mind. Because of this: **Do not enter Daath unless you truly are willing to face all that you are and all that you have done!**

Learning to work at the Daath level of consciousness will awaken the virtue of detachment. Knowledge helps us to control in a detached manner the desires we all have. The person who learns to tap this level will be able to go about their business with a detachment that will prevent distraction. It awakens a strong sense of destiny.

This aspect of Daath can work against us though. it can serve to cut us off from the mainstream of society and people. It can create a kind of misguided fanaticism. It becomes misguided when the other virtues from the tree of Life are not integrated. Those virtues most important to integrate into our life to prevent the unbalanced fanaticism are devotion to the divine, humility, love for fellow humans, and a sense of charity. Detachment should always be from the lower aspects of our personality and not from humanity itself.

On the other hand, Daath will open us to higher knowledge. Through it we can awaken a true confidence in the future. It enables us to see across the abyss of our daily lives. We come to *KNOW* that there truly is a better life for us, one that we are capable of creating!

Temple of Daath

WHAT CAN BE ATTAINED THROUGH THIS TEMPLE OF THE MIND:

Hidden knowledge; past life information; creative expression; higher vision and greater perception; knowledge and information that can increase wealth and prosperity; opportunity to balance the male and female aspects of our life; greater clarity of mind; revelation of past life karma.

Symbolized by the magical images and gifts of:
Book of Knowledge, crescent, and pentacle

DIVINE FORCE AVAILABLE: Jehovah Elohim
- Combination of Jah and Jehovah Elohim -
(Creation through Knowledge)

ARCHANGEL MOST ACCESSIBLE: Raphael, Michael, Gabriel,
Auriel
(Archangels of the four directions)

SPIRITS MOST ACCESSIBLE: Serpents of Knowledge
(help us to shift our perceptions)

TOOLS AND IMAGES TO HELP ACCESS THIS LEVEL OF THE MIND:

COLORS:	grays and lavenders
FRAGRANCES:	lilac, bay oil, wisteria
MEDITATION STONE:	Herkimer diamond, fluorite
ASTROLOGY:	Sirius, the Dog Star
MAGICAL IMAGE:	Janus type figure (man with 2 faces, looking in opposite directions); an Isis figure

WEAKNESSES THAT HINDER DAATH'S POTENTIALS:
doubts; fears, fanaticism; apathy and blame

STRENGTHS THAT ASSIST DAATH'S POTENTIALS:
open-mindedness; willingness to face karma; courage to express

We live in a time
in which
supersensible knowledge
can no longer remain
the secret possession of a few
but must become
common property
of all those in whom
the sense for life in this age
stirs as a need
for their soul's existence.

- Rudolph Steiner

Chapter Five

Hidden Temple of Daath

There are two primary rules to keep in mind when working with Daath. The first is: **Do not perform Daath exercises too frequently.** With most exercises with the Qabala, I often recommend they be performed three days in a row. Three is a creative number and its rhythm amplifies the effects of the exercise we are performing. With Daath, perform the exercise **ONCE, and then leave at least a month after working it so you can truly discern the effects on your life!**

Work with Daath in small doses. Our bodily systems and our individual lives must be able to assimilate the experience of Daath with all of its archetypal force. To explore Daath without creating imbalances requires time and patience. Knowledge without true understanding or the wisdom of how to apply it for the benefit of all is very dangerous. It takes time to reassimilate and integrate the increased knowledge and awareness in the most beneficial manner.

Too much, too soon will overwhelm and create a collapse or fall within our own lives. If knowledge is to be used correctly, we must be able to discern how it affects us individually and how it can affect everyone and everything else in the universe. Treating this cardinal rule too lightly is what causes the sharp, serpent bite of knowledge.

The second cardinal rule is: **Only explore Daath if you are truly able and willing to handle the responsibility**

and repercussions (good and bad). Knowledge is often given as the cause for the fall of humanity, as depicted in the story of Adam and Eve eating the fruit from the Tree of Knowledge. Knowledge has its consequences. If we are to use knowledge, we must be willing to take upon its responsibility.

Touching Daath creates opportunities to learn about ourselves. It can show our darker aspects. Those aspects that we would rather ignore and which can be disruptive to the personality may surface so we can face them and transmute them. Daath is direct. It does not sugarcoat.

Daath can disrupt the conditions of our life with an intensity that can be difficult to rebalance. Here we learn and face true cosmic law. We see what we have done, and we know it must be balanced. For those who have lived many, many lives, karma can be frightening. It is for this reason that many of the ancient, esoteric schools cautioned students against past life exploration. It has the potential of releasing energies that have already been balanced. it can open wounds that have already healed. It can also release the balancing of karma with an intensity that can be agonizing for the soul.

Daath can open a Pandora's Box of past-life karma. The exercise at the end of the chapter can be easily adapted for exploring past lives through Daath, but even with this exercise, caution is recommended. The old saying holds true: **"Be careful of what you ask, for you may get it!"** When we tap Daath, we will get what we ask.

<u>**Caution:**</u>
Do not enter Daath
unless you are willing to face
all that you are and
all that you've done!

Exercise:

The Temple of Knowledge

Benefits:

- knowledge of hidden things
- past life information
- self-examination
- secrets of the universe
- future knowledge
- revelation of personal destiny
- greater knowledge of the Tree of Life

The symbols and images within this exercise have been chosen carefully to elicit the strongest and safest effects from Daath. It is best to familiarize yourself with the meditation and its symbols prior to the working. Contemplating and reflecting upon their significance will help to trigger an even stronger response.

The effects of this exercise are very powerful but very subtle. They will manifest into your daily life in a manner that must be dealt with and transmuted. The exercises work gradually, but it WILL work.

The first time I used this exercise, the effects were felt for months. Old emotions and thoughts arose that had to be dealt with. Numerous individuals commented or inquired about my change in energy. It was not recognized as positive or negative, just different. I discovered information about others that I didn't want to know. I discovered things about me that I did not want to admit.

Knowledge of the self is one of the benefits of this exercise, but knowledge can be painful. It can reveal the thorns in our life that need to be removed. The removal hurts, but in the long run, it is not as painful as allowing a thorn to remain, becoming infected and festering within us.

Remember: **Once you set the energies in motion, they will play themselves out!** If they seem to overwhelm you - and it can happen - the best course of action is to deal with what has been set in motion as best as you are able at the time. Using the protection and balancing exercises given later can also help. Take a break from working with the Tree of Life. Focus on the daily, mundane activities for a few weeks or longer. Spend a lot of time in nature; it will help ground the energies released and help keep you balanced as well.

The wonderful thing about Daath though is that anything cleaned out through knowledge of the self will be replaced by something much more beneficial to us. We find ourselves propelled along a higher destiny. Through it we enhance our learning in every other area of life. Through Daath we learn to read from the Holy Writ - the Book of Knowledge of the universe.

Knowledge can be painful, especially since it can be used to interfere with the free will of others. A misuse of knowledge draws to us strong repercussions. Through this exercise, you will have the opportunity to open to Daath - to open to knowledge, to read from the book of your life - past, present and future.

Preparing for the Exercise

Before performing this exercise, make some preparations:

1. Familiarize yourself with Daath and all of its symbols and energies. This includes the sigils on the following page.

Sigils of the Archangels

Raphael (Eastern Quarter)

Gabriel (Western Quarter)

Michael (Southern Quarter)

Auriel (Northern Quarter)

The sigils are symbolic signatures of the four great archangels. They are based upon Golden Dawn techniques of applying Hebrew letters to the ancient symbol of the Rose and Rose Cross. There are many ways of forming the signatures of these beings; this is only one. For a complete elaboration, you can refer to *THE GOLDEN DAWN* by Israel Regardie (Llewellyn Publications, 1986; p.9-47).

These sigils in Daath (and in the Daath exercise) serve to balance the expression of knowledge within our lives. Any meditation or work with Daath should utilize the sigils or other symbols/images of the four great archangels. They provide strong protection and grounding of the energies awakened in Daath.

2. Make sure you will be undisturbed.

3. Review the benefits and precautions.

4. Set the tone with the appropriate fragrance, candle, etc. Although with many meditations music can be a wonderful aid, for working with Daath, no music is usually most beneficial.

5. Perform a progressive relaxation.

This exercise is a guide. Do not worry about remembering all of the details. We must use our own insight and allow the basic imagery to adapt them to us. At first hold as closely as possible to the scenario. Once familiar with it, it can be adapted more freely. Each may find their own variations occurring.

There will be different responses to this exercise, but once the temple is opened - as it is through this exercise - then we can go back and read from the Book of Knowledge. This book can open us to knowledge on almost anything we wish to learn - especially if we are ready for it. Keep in mind that someone who does not know basic mathematics will not be able to perform calculus. The knowledge that opens to us will be that for which we are prepared.

Every reading of the book does have its accompanying bite, usually at the end. (It will vary from individual to individual.) The pain of the bite varies according to what knowledge is being revealed and its potential for misuse. The bite is our reminder that misused knowledge has its price!

The time frame in which to work this exercise and experience results varies. It could take as long as a month to recognize the effects, but usually it takes no more than a day or so for the first confirmations to make themselves known. It usually comes through new revelations, new opportunities for knowledge, discovery of hidden things going on around us, or a variety of other possibilities. Pay attention to what reveals itself to you in the days following the exercise.

The ancient mystery schools taught their students to "KNOW THYSELF". This is the kind of energy released through this exercise. It releases the energy that stimulates and awakens insight into ourselves and our lives. It releases energy to help us see aspects of ourselves and our lives that we have not seen or not seen as clearly as we should. It helps manifest conditions that enable us to have knowledge of ourselves and of things affecting ourselves - good and bad.

It is usually best to wait a month before repeating this exercise, but it is only a guideline, especially upon its initial working. The month period enables us to determine the effect that this exercise will likely have on our life. This requires some self-examination.

In the days that follow this exercise, ask yourself some questions:

- Have your emotions been more charged or volatile since performing the exercise?
- Have new situations arisen - good and/or bad?
- How are you relating to people in your life or they to you since the exercise?
- Are there certain things upsetting you more?
- Have new learning opportunities (formal & informal) presented themselves?
- Have new people come into your life? What are they like?
- Are you having things revealed - good and/or bad?

Examine every aspect of your life. Remember that knowledge throws light upon shadows. It forces us to look at things from a different perspective. Suspicions may be clarified. Secrets may be revealed. Hidden insights may occur.

Self-knowledge is most important. Unless we can become aware of those aspects of us that limit us, we can never clean them out and replace them with energies that are more beneficial. This exercise sets energy in motion to bring out new perspectives on ourselves. This will happen in both obvious and subtle ways. Thus we need some time to assimilate what has been released into our life or we may bring on too many learning circumstances too quickly. When that occurs, the learning is disruptive rather than healing. this is why some time be given before repeating this exercise.

Use your own judgment. Remember that the Qabala will show us our greatest strengths and our greatest weaknesses. If not controlled, especially when working with Daath, this can be troublesome. If you find yourself going to Daath to find out things for which you have no direct use, to intrude into the privacy of others or to satisfy some unbalanced urge for gossip, there will be a price!

There is with most people a craving for more knowledge. It must always be balanced. Those who have much often want more. Those who have access to much often want it opened and augmented, even at the risk of imbalance. There are times to seek and use knowledge, and there are times when it is best to leave it alone. There is an old axiom: "A little knowledge can be a dangerous thing." When we work with Daath, the truth of this axiom can manifest.

The autonomy of the individual must be recognized unqualifyingly. No one has the right to use knowledge to impinge the free will of another or to over ride it. Free will is one of the greatest gifts humanity has received, and it does have its responsibilities and consequences. To use knowledge inappropriately to impinge upon anyone's free will has dire consequences.

Through Daath and through what unfolds within your life after accessing it, we learn that knowledge is most powerful when it is used to serve!

Entering the Temple of Daath

You are standing outside the ancient tree of life. As always, its immense size astounds you. It grows larger and more impressive with each visit. Today though there is a heightened sense of anticipation and anxiousness. It is the first day of school as far as you are concerned.

The Temple of Daath - the Temple of Knowledge - is something you have looked forward to for a long time. To be able to finally know! To have the knowledge of all the ages at your hands - what joy! Knowledge has done so much good and yet caused so much pain, and a temple that encompasses all knowledge fills you with a sense of wonder.

Humans know so much about the physical world, and so little about other worlds and dimensions. Humans can be arrogant. Humans like to believe that no one knows more or better. Fanatics have always believed they knew better than the ordinary person. History books are filled with such individuals and the chaos they create. Knowledge entails responsibility and it requires continual discernment.

You see the opening at the base of the tree. You take a deep breath and then bend slightly, stepping into the now familiar darkness. You are not sure that you know how to open this temple, so you breathe deeply, relaxing.

As the darkness of the inner tree encloaks you, you here a soft whispered voice.

"What is it you seek?"

Startled at such a voice within your tree, you are unsure how to respond. The voice speaks softly again.

"What is it you seek?"

You are a little confused. Have you done something wrong? And you cannot answer because you do not know the answer.

A third time the voice speaks the question.

"What is it you seek?"

Your mind races, knowing there must be a correct response. Then as if from some primordial remembrance, the words come forth. Though you speak them softly, hesitantly, they echo in the hollows of the tree with great power.

"I seek to know that I may serve."

A dim light begins to grow inside the tree. You wait, your breath becoming a bit more rapid in anticipation. You remind yourself to be patient - that a long awaited dream is about to be fulfilled.

As the light grows, a stone gray, nearly empty room is revealed. Your eyes widen and your shoulders sink in disappointment. This can not be the Temple of Knowledge!

You had come expecting the magnificence of the libraries of Alexandria, and you find only an empty room. No books. No scrolls. No writings or markings of any kind, except for insignias carved into the upper part of each of the four walls. Each is different and somewhat familiar, but they tell you nothing. It makes no sense. And you are filled with disappointment.

There is not even an altar in this temple - if in deed it is a temple. Near the back of the room sits a wooden pedestal. Its base is in the shape of a pentagram and three rods upward out of it to a crescent-shaped surface. Upon this crescent surface sits a large leather-bound volume. On either side of the middle rod of the pedestal are two stone carved snakes, resting in a circular coil on the pentagram base.

As you step forward to the pedestal, the surface with the book is chest level - heart level to you.

"We enter the mysteries through the sphere of the mind, but only so we can worship at the shrine in the heart."

It is the same voice as before, but its sound softly echoes in your mind and in the air around you. You are not sure if they are your own words from some deep level of your own consciousness or the words of some being that you have not yet discovered. It is very puzzling indeed.

"It is good that you are puzzled, for the asking of the question is the beginning of the answer."

The voice rings again. You look about to search the shadows, but there are no shadows! There is dim lighting at best within this room, but there are no shadows! It is as if they have been chased away. There are no blacks or whites. Only grays.

You turn slowly back to the pedestal, a little disoriented. But a part of you knows that new knowledge can change the world. Above the book burns a pine cone shaped lamp that provides the only light within the temple. You know that it must have significance, but it eludes you at the moment.

You focus your attention on the large volume. It is closed, wrapped in a leather binding that is strapped and locked. You reach out gingerly to touch it. Your fingers brush it softly, lightly. You feel its texture, and your hand traces the image of a man with two faces looking into opposite directions. As you touch the image the lamp grows brighter.

You fumble with the latch, and it pops open. You lean forward, preparing to open the volume. You lay it wide, like wings across the pedestal top. And there on the top of the very first page is your name.

You stare with utter surprises and disbelief. You fail to notice in your surprise that the coiled snakes have shimmered into life. They slide upward, crisscrossing and intertwining around the middle rod of the pedestal. Slowly they begin to climb toward the book.

As you lean forward to read what is written about you in this book, the heads of the snakes appear around the sides. Before you can respond to their appearance, the twin serpents strike - biting you on the temple behind the eyes. You jump back, drawing your hands to your face, feeling a quick sharp pain piercing your entire head.

The book snaps closed with your movement. You watch, eyes wide, as the serpents draw back, receding down that middle rod to settle once more at the base. There they shimmer once more into stone. The pain in the temple disappears, and all that is left is a soft, soothing tingling to remind you what has occurred.

"The first bite of true knowledge is always the hardest to bear and catches one off guard."

You look around the room in amazement. Everything is brighter, more distinct. The bites from the serpents of knowledge have somehow cleared your eyesight. The insignias on the walls begin to glow, casting the grays back and filling the temple with crystalline white light. For a brief moment you see the images of four great beings overlaying the insignias. The four great archangels!

As the images fade upon your recognition, the temple begins to shake and vibrate as if to collapse upon it. You fall to the ground, curling up and covering your head in fear. The temple roars!

Then nothing! Everything stills. There is silence.

You are lying upon the floor. You have no idea how long you have been there. You shiver and realize that you are completely naked. You draw yourself up slowly, confused and bewildered.

"All knowledge has its price, but its blessing is greater than any discomfort. By opening to it, you can strip away the old. You can tear down the old foundations so that the new may be laid. Only then does new light and life enter in forever. Knowledge brings light only when it is balanced with love. Knowledge is only painful if we don't use it to serve. Knowledge with love will create a new world."

The voice fades again. All is quiet, but something is different. Why does the room feel so strange? Why is it so much more crystalline? You pause to listen for the voice.

Nothing.

Silence is your only answer.

You turn to leave. You glance back once more to the pedestal. The pine cone lamp brightens in response. The book lays itself open for you. A soft breeze moves through the temple, passing through you and filling you. You feel energized, healed, strong and balanced.

The breeze flips the pages of the book. You smile, beginning to understand. A part of you knows that the Book of Knowledge is now open to you once more. In it you will be able to read from your past, the present and the future.

You feel alive and more in control of your life and what is to unfold than ever before. It's as if a part of you knows that all is needed for you will reveal it. The future is something to look forward to, not run from. You know that it is there for you to create in any manner that you choose.

You step from the Tree of Life, and as the inner visions fade, they do so only to be born into the outer life. You breathe deeply, your heart and mind at rest, secure in the knowledge that awaits you!

We need not be aware of the inner world. We do not realize its existence most of the time. But many people enter it - unfortunately without guides, confusing the outer with inner realities and the inner with the outer - and generally lose their capacity to function competently in ordinary relations.

This need not be so. The process of entering the other world from this world and returning to this world from the other world is as natural as death and giving birth or being born...

Among physicians and priests there should be some who are guides, who can educt the person from this world and induct him to the other, to guide him in it and to lead him back again.

One who enters the other world by breaking a shell - or through a door - through a partition - the curtains part or rise and a veil is lifted.

The outer divorced from any illumination from the inner is in a state of darkness - an age of darkness.

- RD Laing
Politics of Experience

Part III -

The Secret
of
Pathworking

Chapter Six

The Secret of Pathworking

There are 22 paths that connect the temples of the Tree of Life in its traditional teachings. And there are other paths that are hidden, and which will be covered later in this book. In fact, these hidden paths have never been explored in any written text on the Qabala. While the 22 traditional paths are bridges between the various levels of the subconscious (the sephiroth), the hidden paths enable us to take some short cuts in accessing certain levels but they have their own dangers, as well as benefits. Ideally, paths enable us to access any level of the mind at any time to any degree we desire. The problem is that these bridges may be blocked and not fully functional, inhibiting a full and powerful access to various levels of the consciousness and some of our greatest potentials. When any of the paths are unblocked, they become true paths of wisdom.

One of the most effective means of developing our potentials and unblocking the bridges between levels of our subconscious mind is through *PATHWORKING*. Pathworking is the process of using archetypal symbols and images in an imaginative (and sometimes mythologized) journey to elicit specific effects within our daily lives and to open the psychic and spiritual planes more consciously. It can be accomplished through a variety of meditative and ceremonial techniques. Pathworking is a magical use of creative imagination.

Most creative visualizations are a type of pathworking. Daydreams can be a type of pathworking as well. Pathworking is the use of the symbols and images in an imaginative journey for a wide variety of purposes. We can walk a magical path or take a magical journey for healing, for divination, for enlightenment or even to examine symbols and images for clarification.

The problem though with many types of pathworkings is that the effects they elicit within our daily life are not easily defined. They are atavistic - uncontrolled. Rarely are there guidelines or maps that reveal how the energies and symbols we focus upon are likely to play out within our lives.

This is what makes pathworking with Qabalistic imagery so powerful. The symbols and images have been used in very similar ways by great numbers of people for a great many centuries. Because of this, we know what effects such meditations and workings are likely to have within our life. We can then work with them to elicit specifically what we wish and need.

Qabalistic pathworking is an imaginative journey between two of the temples on the Tree of Life. On this journey various symbols, images and magickal gifts are encountered, according to the effects we wish to elicit. This activates and releases specific archetypal energies into our daily life. These energies manifest life situations that bring rewards, tests, enlightenment that accelerate our own spiritual development.

A great mystique has developed in modern times surrounding this occult practice of pathworking. For many groups and individuals it is perceived as the be-all and end-all of metaphysical skills. The truth is that there are variations of pathworkings performed at some time by most people who meditate and who practice spiritual development in any of its many forms.

Pathworking is simply a tool for opening and expanding awareness. It is a meditation technique that incorporates very specific guided imagery, archetypal symbols, creative visualization and imagination to open new dimensions and realities. Pathworking is sometimes viewed as the means to manifesting our most wonderful innate gifts - as the epitome of spiritual unfoldment. It is seen as the pot of gold at the end of the rainbow, but this is somewhat misleading. It is a technique that merely opens a pathway to the pot of gold. That pathway must still be traveled. We must also remember throughout the journey that the Qabala will show us our greatest potentials while also revealing our greatest weaknesses. It will manifest our greatest rewards and bring upon our greatest tests.

The Benefits of Pathworking

It is very easy in the modern world to think we know all about the world and its various realms. After all, explorers have touched the four corners of the Earth. We have ventured into space and into the ocean depths. Others are just now beginning to explore the more subtle realms and dimensions of life, realms that have served as the inspiration to most of our ancient myths, legends and archetypes.

Reading about these realms and experiencing them are two entirely different things. We cannot truly know something until we have experienced it. Theory and knowledge without application is impotent. To most people our legends, myths and ancient teachings are merely words, but there is a means to discovering the truths and realities upon which they are based. One of the most powerful means of discovering the truths is through pathworking.

The paths on the Tree of Life are keys for astral travel, scrying in the spirit, past life exploration, healing and more. They traverse the mind and the various planes of existence. By traveling or working the paths, we awaken dormant and untapped resources of the mind. We open channels to the conscious mind.

Although pathworking may seem like a fantasy of

the mind or an innocuous daydream, it is dangerous to assume they will have little effect upon our lives. We are working with powerful symbols which generate and release archetypal forces. The paths contain symbols that will act upon the subconscious mind and awaken what is hidden there. And although the situations, experiences and workings may be symbolic, they will strongly affect the physical world in which we operate daily.

We must remember that whatever we do on one level of our consciousness will flow down and manifest similar expressions on a more mundane level. We are learning to use symbols and images to activate and experience specific energies within our life. This occurs through the normal, day-to-day circumstances. Those who doubt that such connections and relationships exist have only intellectualized the process, and these individuals will come face-to-face with what will be for them a harsh reality of the interrelationship.

The Qabala is a system of personal evolution. Through pathworkings we instigate energies that will in turn manifest situations and experiences that hasten our growth. It makes us face what we have not faced. It brings to the surface our hidden fears so that we have no choice but to confront and overcome them. In this way we open more fully to higher and stronger knowledge and spiritual experiences. Because of this, those who approach the Qabala lightly or wish to dabble will experience a strong awakening.

It has been said that the Qabala will show us our deepest fears, but it will also show us our greatest potentials. Through pathworking we become the catalysts of our own lives. By working the paths, we begin the process of consciously and willingly finding the dross of our lives and then clearing it out to reveal the light within. Pathworking brings upon us situations and activates those stresses that must be dealt with for change to occur.

The Qabala is an agent for transformation between the inner and the outer, the upper and the lower, the past and the future and for all levels of consciousness. The raising of matter and awareness from an ordinary level to one that is extraordinary is the task of the true Seeker. And although difficult at times, the epiphanies that come from each activation and working are worth every difficulty.

Without techniques like pathworking, the tasks and the successes of the seeker are often random and atavistic. The conscious work upon the Tree of Life enables us to have a system that we can adapt and use effectively for ourselves.

I must stress though that some preparation is needed. We should at the very least be somewhat familiar with the energies of the individual sephiroth and worked with each one of them several times before undertaking pathworking. Remember that the sephiroth hold traces of energies from all paths that enter or leave them. Thus every level of consciousness - every sephiroth - contains not only its own unique aspects, but it also contains influences from all of connecting paths to them.

Pathworking links two sephiroth, activating both of their individual energies, along with the path's own aspects. Thus, before a pathworking is performed, the work on each individual sephira should precede. When it comes to the Qabala, more is not better, and the goal is to learn how the energies will play themselves out within our life without being overwhelmed by them. In this way all of the benefits are achieved more easily and more successfully.

Phenomena of Pathworking

The symbols we use to bridge and create doorways between the levels of our mind, also serve to create bridges and doorways to other realms of life. Thus, in the process of working with the Tree of Life, we begin to experience a great increase in psychic and astral phenomena. Dreams become more colorful, lucid and even prophetic. Our own psychic sensibilities will become heightened, manifesting in a variety of ways.

This is why pathworking is so powerful. It not only bridges the various levels of consciousness within us, but it opens bridges between our mundane world and the less substantial dimensions (the spiritual worlds) operating around us. When this occurs, we cannot deny the reality of some divine force within the universe.

Psychic/Astral Phenomena of Pathworking

1. Mediumship
2. Apportation
3. Materialization
4. Precipitation
5. Clairvoyance
6. Clairsentience
7. Levitation
8. Spirit Lights
9. Fire handling
10. Transmutation of metals
11. Production of fire
12. Psychic and spiritual healings
13. Spirit communications
14. Animal and nature communication
15. Lucid dreaming

Pathworking and

The ancient Qabalists knew that if we tried to explore the subtler dimensions, we could open ourselves to wide barrage of energies that might not be controlled. Because of this, they explored the universe in a very controlled and directed manner, using the Tree of Life diagram as their map. The various images and symbols became road markers, guiding them from one level of consciousness to the next, assisting them in finding their way through it. The images and symbols are keys to the astral dimension and the subtle forces that permeate all of our lives - often without us being aware. These images, symbols, colors and various correspondences help us in four distinct ways as we become spiritual explorers through the Qabalistic Tree of Life:

1. They exercise our psychic and spiritual muscles.

Many times our spiritual and psychic muscles - just like our physical muscles - will atrophy if we do not use them. The work with the various symbols and images, along with exercises like that which follows in this chapter, serve to exercise these abilities. They stir our psychic muscle circulation. They stretch our abilities, loosening them and strengthening them. They restore the flow of blood, so to speak, so we can awaken, use and control our spiritual and psychic muscles and potentials more effectively.

2. They open and close astral doorways, prevent our getting lost among the subtleties and ever-changing energies of the astral dimensions.

When we open to the Tree of Life and the other dimensions permeating it, the symbols, images and correspondences help us to keep track of where we are. They protect us from accidentally wandering off our path or work with the Tree. Sometimes new images will show

the Spiritual Explorer

up, but if they are not in conjunction with those with which we are familiar and with which we are working, it is very often an indicator we have wandered off track. By focusing upon the image and symbol we have chosen - or by using the divine names of the path we are working - we dissipate any intrusive forces, and we create a doorway back to our correct location. They provide a built in safety line.

3. They also help us to open and clear the pathways between the different levels of consciousness.

The symbols and images often act like faucets by which we can control the flow of energy into our normal, waking consciousness. Through them, we learn to turn the energy on and off at will. Work with pathworking symbols and images can be compared to cleaning out clogged pipes or pruning out the dead limbs and leaves of a Tree. Our own psychic/spiritual pipes may be clogged with misconceptions, misinformation, fears, doubts, and limitations (self-imposed or otherwise). We, as a living Tree, may find ourselves smothering from stunted growth and dead limbs. By working with the Tree and its images, we clean out the pipes and shake loose the debris to restore to the Tree (ourselves) greater flow. In turn, we then have more freedom and ability to stretch and grow fuller.

4. They assist us in accessing specific forces within ourselves and the universe.

The symbols and images open doors to ever-deepening levels of consciousness and ever-increasing new realms and dimensions. The various correspondences for the sephiroth and the paths are ways of controlling and directing the manifestations of these energies and dimensions within our lives.

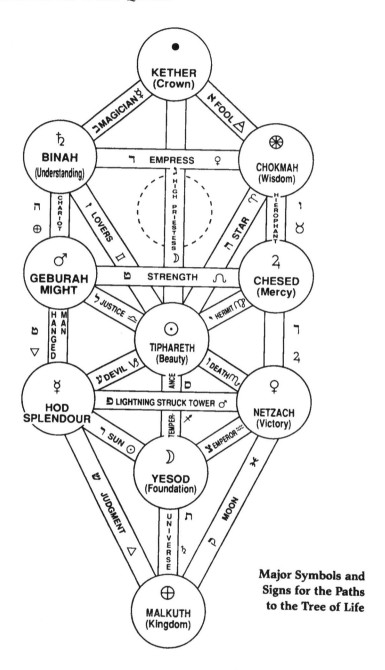

Major Symbols and
Signs for the Paths
to the Tree of Life

The more symbols and images we use in the pathworking, the stronger the effects upon us in our daily life. If we use less - keeping it simpler - the effects will be less intense and often more easily recognized and handled.

Symbols and Images of Pathworking

At first the symbols and images may seem too complicated and intricate, there being so many symbols and images associated with the Tree of Life. This is where a journal becomes an invaluable tool. The initial work may seem cumbersome, but eventually the use and understanding will grow. We begin to see increasing correspondences, and they begin to teach us aspects of the universe beyond the mundane teachings we have had.

Keep in mind throughout that the work with the symbols reflects powerful archetypal energies. They will stir those archetypal forces up and release them into our daily lives. Through them, we begin to realize that the individual sephiroth are storehouses of our potentials, and the pathworking becomes a generator for setting the energy into motion so we can unfold those potentials.

As we work with the pathworking, energies will be released that will clean out our inner channels. It will point out where the bridges need to be repaired. *The energy will manifest in a myriad of ways according to how we use the symbols and images.* The symbols and images are keys but we must still find our own way of using them within our life. That is part of the responsibility of the true spiritual explorer. And it begins with learning to use them as keys to open the spiritual doors to human potentials and other dimensions.

The Key Symbols

As with the ten sephiroth or temples, there are many associations with the various paths. Each path has symbols, magical images and gifts, colors, astrological and tarot correspondences and a variety of other symbolic associations. All of these can affect us in the same manner that the symbols and images for each temple can affect us. They are links to archetypal forces. When they are used in a specific meditative or ceremonial manner - such as in pathworking - they elicit specific effects that will play themselves out within our physical lives.

The path descriptions that follow provide guidelines for the major symbols, images and keynotes. For each, there is a spiritual experience, and a life path keynote. In chapter seven, we will examine how to determine which of the paths of wisdom is our life path - a path whose lessons and potentials are most important to us in this lifetime.

Three of the other correspondences given are most important, in that they reflect the primary energies of the path and hold the key to creating astral doorways that we can use. The remaining correspondences provide tools for fine tuning what is activated within our lives through the exercises provided.

1. The Hebrew Letter

The first symbol is the Hebrew letter. The esoteric aspects of alphabets hold the key to many mysteries of life. In their simplest aspects, the shape of the letter, its meaning and other associations with it have significance. In the Tree of Life, the Hebrew letters are a potent reflection of the essence of the path. This text will not explore all of the significances of the paths. It is just a starting point. For in depth work, refer to my earlier book *More Simplified Magic*.

The ancient Hebrew alphabet, one of the forerunners of our own, has great mystical significance. There is not space within this text to cover all of the subtleties, but in essence each letter has a numerical significance, color attribution and other symbolism. A study of esoteric linguistics will reveal much more.

2. Astrological Influence

The second most important correspondence with the path is its astrological sign. The astrological aspects of the path reflect some of the cosmic energy that will be released into our lives (or stimulated more strongly) through ourwork with the particular path. The stars and planets can have an influence upon us, although is subtle. A study of astrology can provide some insight into some of the

Tree of Life & the Hebrew Letters

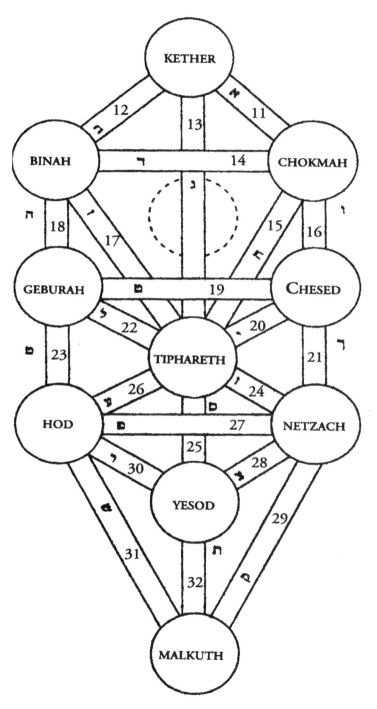

subtle influences of the path.

The glyph (symbol) for each of the signs of the zodiac, planets and elements can be a powerful tool for opening psychic doorways. As we will examine in part three, an examination of the path associated with your personal astrological sign can provide some wonderful insight into your own potentials, strengths and weaknesses.

3. Tarot Designation

The third most important correspondence is the tarot card of the path. Tarot cards are pictorial reflections of spiritual and physical patterns and energies at play. And like the other two primary symbols, they can be powerful doorways into the more subtle realms of life. Yes, there can be differences as to which card applies to which path. Those given are the more commonly accepted.

The tarot images reflect certain archetypal forces. That and the thoughtform energy that has developed around them through the centuries of use make them powerful bridges. The 22 cards of the major arcana reflect the energies inherent to the paths of the Tree. They also reflect the combined energies of the Sephiroth they link.

4. Benefits, Strengths and Weaknesses

For each path there are primary benefits that can unfold from pathworking, along with the strengths and weaknesses that can be achieved and revealed. These are traditionally referred to as vices and virtues. These are strengths and weaknesses within us, but they can reflect strengths and weaknesses of others in our life or qualities likely to show up in various endeavors within our life.

5. Other Correspondences

For each path there are other correspondences and associations. The color rings the doorbell of the level of our mind appropriate for our task. Color has a great potential to affect us physically and spiritually. There are also magical gifts with each path as there are with each temple. We bring these gifts out of the Tree of Life with us after the pathworking. These gifts represent the positive benefits that will unfold in your life as a result of the pathworking.

Performing a Simple Pathworking

1. Decide on a path and study its qualities and symbols. Think of it as a Temple to Temple visitation or crossing.

2. Enter into the first sephira of the path and call the temple into being as you learned earlier.

3. Once the temple has formed around you, imagine a door behind the altar. The door can be anything you wish. Some people use a life size image of the appropriate tarot card and just step into the scenery (and then out of it at the other sephira). Some just imagine a door engraved with the symbols of the path.

4. As you step through, you find yourself upon a path to the other temple, which you see in the distance. The path is in the appropriate color. You are joined by one of the Archangels of the two sephira of the path.

5. As you walk along the path, you encounter things appropriate to the path. You find the gifts or what symbolizes those gifts.

6. Halfway through the journey, you find a road marker. I like to use the image of the Hebrew Letter or the astrological symbol for the path. I imagine finding it hanging from a tree, in the form of a necklace that I will put on and wear through the journey and leave beside the path before I walk into the second temple.

7. Step from the path through a similar door as in the beginning. And call the 2nd temple into being. Take a few moments to reflect on what this working will unfold for you. Then thank the Archangels for their assistance.

8. Speak the divine name for the first temple, followed by that of the second. Repeat three times as the temples and the path fade from the vision and close. You leave the temples and path behind, bringing their energies out into your daily life.

32nd Path – Malkuth to Yesod

Spiritual Experience:
Vision of the Holy Guardian Angel and Vision of the Machinery of the Universe

Life Path Keynote:
Awakening to your true spirit

Primary Symbols:

Hebrew Letter:	Tau (the cross)
Astrological Influence:	Saturn
Tarot Designation:	The World Card
Colors:	Indigo and Black
Magical gifts:	Cauldron and the girdle

Pathworking Benefits:
Overcomes depression, awakens intuition, dreamwork, strengthens the light body, astral projection

Strengths Achieved:
Discrimination, independence, motivation, facing fears, common sense, self-discipline, groundedness

Weaknesses Revealed:
Greed, idleness, depression, lack of discipline, hidden fears, lack of feeling, depression

31st Path – Malkuth to Hod

Spiritual Experience:
Vision of the Holy Guardian Angel and Splendor

Life Path Keynote:
Power of Relationships

Primary Symbols:

Hebrew Letter:	Shin (the tooth)
Astrological Influence:	Fire
Tarot Designation:	Judgment
Colors:	Orange and Scarlet
Magical Gifts:	Flint and Steel

Pathworking Benefits:
Energy for transformation, relationships clarified, idealism, opportunity for renewal, truths revealed, balance of give and take

Strengths Achieved:
Discrimination, truth, strength of will, fortitude, self-discovery; helpfulness & kindness, inspiration

Weaknesses Revealed:
Avarice, dishonesty, weak willed, fear of change, ruthlessness, irresponsibility, inertia

30th Path – Yesod to Hod

Spiritual Experience:
Vision of the Splendor of the Universe and its Machinery

Life Path Keynote:
Vision and Enlightenment

Primary Symbols:

Hebrew Letter:	Resh (head)
Astrological Influence:	Sun
Tarot Designation:	The Sun Card
Colors:	Orange
Magical Gifts:	Lion and Sparrow hawk

Pathworking Benefits:
Healing, enlightenment, artistic inspiration, prophecy, insight into alchemy

Strengths Achieved:
Recognition of purpose, optimism, self-mastery, power in healing, balance of reason & intuition

Weaknesses Revealed:
Selfishness, fears, lack of diligence, ego-centricism, overly rational, idleness, dishonesty

29th Path – Malkuth to Netzach

Spiritual Experience:
Vision of the Holy Guardian Angel and Beauty Triumphant

Life Path Keynote:
Creative Power of Sexuality

Primary Symbols:

Hebrew Letter:	Qoph (back of the head)
Astrological Influence:	Pisces
Tarot Designation:	The Moon
Colors:	Crimson
Magical Gifts:	Scarab, Dolphin

Pathworking Benefits: Creativity, scrying abilities, attunement to animals and nature, increased sexuality, discrimination

Strengths Achieved: Unselfishness, simplicity, faith, family harmony, innovation, understanding animals and nature

Weaknesses Revealed: Greed, ungoverned imagination, sexual obsession, separatism, excessive empathy, withdrawal

28th Path – Yesod to Netzach

Spiritual Experience:
Vision of the Machinery of the Universe and Beauty Triumphant

Life Path Keynote:
Dreams and Inspiration

Primary Symbols:

Hebrew Letter:	Tzaddi (fishhook)
Astrological Influence:	Aquarius
Tarot Designation:	The Star (sometimes The Emperor)
Colors:	Violet
Magical Gifts:	Grail, Star, Apple, Eagle

Pathworking Benefits:
Creative and sexual power, higher aspirations, peacefulness, loyalty, dream opportunities, unselfishness and independence

Strengths Achieved:
Hope and inspiration, individuality, strength to follow dreams, greater will and understanding

Weaknesses Revealed:
Fear of following dreams, pettiness, self-doubt, impracticality; imposition of will, lust, and idleness

27th Path – Hod to Netzach

Spiritual Experience:
Vision of Splendor and Vision of Beauty

Life Path Keynote:
Endurance, Courage and Faith

Primary Symbols:

Hebrew Letter:	Peh (mouth)
Astrological Influence:	Mars
Tarot Designation:	The Tower
Colors:	Scarlet
Magical Gifts:	Lightning, rubies, wolf and bear

Pathworking Benefits:
Cleansing; tearing down of old; courage and faith; balancing of psychic energies; endurance; change of fortunes

Strengths Achieved:
Endurance; courage; faith, self-awareness; fighting spirit; clarifying changes; truth

Weaknesses Revealed:
Emotional & mental conflicts; insecurities; self-delusion; feelings of being lost; imbalances

26th Path – Hod to Tiphareth

Spiritual Experience:
Vision of Splendor and Harmony

Life Path Keynote:
Faith in a Higher Power

Primary Symbols:

Hebrew Letter:	Ayin (eye)
Astrological Influence:	Capricorn
Tarot Designation:	The Devil
Colors:	Indigo
Magical Gifts:	Yoni and lingam; the ass

Pathworking Benefits:
Truth; devotion; practicality; loyalty; trust; awareness of the needs of others; stronger inner voice

Strengths Achieved:
Strength of will; tolerance; pragmatism; stronger belief system; openness & innocence

Weaknesses Revealed:
Weak-willed; false pride; selfishness; dishonesty; conceit; domineering & demanding

25th Path – Yesod to Tiphareth

Spiritual Experience:
Vision of the Universe in Harmony

Life Path Keynote:
Power of Choice and Vision

Primary Symbols:

Hebrew Letter:	Samech (prop)
Astrological Influence:	Sagittarius
Tarot Designation:	Temperance
Colors:	Blue
Magical Gifts:	Rainbow; bow and arrow; bridge

Pathworking benefits:
Rebirth; self-sufficiency; astral projection; higher forms of psychism; understanding; devotion

Strengths Achieved:
Self-sufficiency; responsibility; harmony; self-discovery; boldness; moderation

Weaknesses Revealed:
Temptations; irresponsibility; fear of choosing; gluttony; exaggeration; narrow-sightedness

24th Path – Netzach to Tiphareth

Spiritual Experience:
Vision of Beauty and Harmony

Life Path Keynote:
Death and Rebirth

Primary Symbols:

Hebrew Letter:	Nun (fish)
Astrological Influence:	Scorpio
Tarot Designation:	Death
Colors:	Green Blue
Magical Gifts:	Boat; phoenix; eagle

Pathworking Benefits:
Transformation and rebirth; devotion; unselfishness; facing of fears; healing; new & deeper friendships; opening to new possibilities

Strengths Achieved:
Acceptance; assimilation of grief; understanding of other's problems; ability to leave past behind

Weaknesses Revealed:
Fear of change; inability to understand others; seductiveness; misuse of friendships; egotism

23rd Path – Hod to Geburah

Spiritual Experience:
Vision of Splendor and Power

Life Path Keynote:
Revelation and Blossoming of Power

Primary Symbols:

Hebrew Letter:	Mem (water)
Astrological Influence:	Element of Water
Tarot Designation:	The Hanged Man
Colors:	Deep Blue
Magical Gifts:	Cup & sacramental wine; clay pots

Pathworking Benefits:
Truth and courage; new perspectives; clarifying emotions; upliftment; opportunities for new visions; heightened sensitivities and instincts; discovery of life purpose

Strengths Achieved:
Tolerance; upliftment; compassion; sensitivity; greater service; trust of instincts; discernment

Weaknesses Revealed:
Intolerance; depression; focus on material; self indulgence; dominance; overly impressionable

22nd Path – Tiphareth to Geburah

Spiritual Experience:
Vision of Harmony and Power

Life Path Keynote:
Justice and Karmic Adjustments

Primary Symbols:

Hebrew Letter:	Lamed (ox goad)
Astrological Influence:	Libra
Tarot Designation:	Justice
Colors:	Emerald Green
Magical Gifts:	Scales; feather; spider & elephant

Pathworking Benefits:
Justice & karmic adjustments; courage; balance; artistic creativity; forgiveness; revelation of consequences

Strengths Achieved:
Application of thought & energy; developing conscience; decisiveness; impartiality; objectivity

Weaknesses Revealed:
Duality; unforgiving; failure to make decisions; deceitfulness; lack of conscience; ignoring our disruptions; superficiality

21st Path – Netzach to Chesed

Spiritual Experience:
Vision of Beauty and Love

Life Path Keynote:
Call of the Quest and the Fates

Primary Symbols:

Hebrew Letter:	Kaph (palm of hand)
Astrological Influence:	Jupiter
Tarot Designation:	Wheel of Fortune
Colors:	Violet
Magical Gifts:	The Golden Fleece; the grail

Pathworking Benefits:
Unselfishness; abundance; new opportunities; hearing the call to the quest; prophecy; understanding of Divine law; practical philosophy and religion

Strengths Achieved:
maturity; commitment; sensibleness; awakening to the Grail; greater effort

Weaknesses Revealed:
Inability to see choices; immaturity; discontent; non-committal; self-pity; chronic complaining

20th Path – Tiphareth to Chesed

Spiritual Experience:
Vision of Harmony and Love

Life Path Keynote:
Visionary Guidance

Primary Symbols:

Hebrew Letter:	Yod (hand)
Astrological Influence:	Virgo
Tarot Designation:	Hermit
Colors:	Yellowish Green
Magical Gifts:	Lamp, wand, Eucharistic host

Pathworking Benefits:
Spiritual guidance; ancient teaching; commitment; helpfulness; service and guidance to others; acceptance of change and of spiritual

Strengths Achieved:
Dependability; unselfishness; openness to change; illumination; strong & silent compassion

Weaknesses Revealed:
Hypocrisy; false pride; non-committal; fear of past; underhandedness; indecisiveness; improper application of power; too much deliberation

19th Path – Geburah to Chesed

Spiritual Experience:
Vision of Power and Love

Life Path Keynote:
Power of Strength of Will

Primary Symbols:

Hebrew Letter:	Teth (serpent)
Astrological Influence:	Leo
Tarot Designation:	Strength
Colors:	Greenish yellow
Magical Gifts:	Cup of bitters; lion and serpent

Pathworking Benefits:
Strength of will; opportunity to burn out dross; self-reliance; courage and obedience to the higher; self-assurance; creativity; self-knowledge

Strengths Achieved:
Peacekeeping ability; righting of wrongs; sincerity; inner alchemy; facing of reality; defense of the weak

Weaknesses Revealed:
Burnt out attitudes; false fronts; avoidance of trials and responsibilities; vanity; indecision; cruelty; taking advantage of others

18th Path – Geburah to Binah

Spiritual Experience:
Vision of Power and Sorrow

Life Path Keynote:
Enlightenment and Birth through Discipline

Primary Symbols:

Hebrew Letter:	Cheth (fence)
Astrological Influence:	Cancer
Tarot Designation:	Chariot
Colors:	Amber
Magical Gifts:	Silver star; sphinx; chariot

Pathworking Benefits:
Protection; will to carry on; hidden knowledge; strengthens psychic energy; enlightenment in darkness; awakens hero's energy

Strengths Achieved:
Balance; enhanced concentration; courage; discipline; self-control; psychic energy

Weaknesses Revealed:
Instability; avarice; cruelty; depletion of energy; lack of caring; inability to focus; no control; lack of determination

17th Path – Tiphareth to Binah

Spiritual Experience:
Vision of harmony and Sorrow

Life Path Keynote:
Fate, Discrimination and Devotion

Primary Symbols:

Hebrew Letter:	Zain (sword)
Astrological Influence:	Gemini
Tarot Designation:	Lovers
Colors:	Orange
Magical Gifts:	Double edged sword; whale; woman crowned with stars; girdle

Pathworking Benefits:
Discrimination; power of silence; devotion to the Great Work; alchemy; balance; love of ourselves

Strengths Achieved:
Versatility; balance of male & female; intelligence; sensitivity; strengthens inner voice; humor

Weaknesses Revealed:
Lack of communication; lack of humor; inability to choose; rigidity; insensitivity; indiscriminate

16th Path - Chesed to Chokmah

Spiritual Experience:
Vision of God's Love, Face-to-Face

Life Path Keynote:
Vision of Incoming Life and Freedom

Primary Symbols:

Hebrew Letter:	Vau (nail)
Astrological Influence:	Taurus
Tarot Designation:	Hierophant
Colors:	Red Orange
Magical Gifts:	Wand; phallus; dove, weddings; bull

Pathworking Benefits:
Initiation into mysteries; obedience to the higher; devotion; uncovering reason for our life; revelation of hidden talents; fertility

Strengths Achieved:
Loyalty; greater understanding; fertility in life; upliftment of the soul; freedom of beliefs; kindness and compassion

Weaknesses Revealed:
false security; ancestral fears; misunderstandings; misplaced loyalties; overindulgence; stubborness; wishy-washy beliefs

15th Path - Tiphareth to Chokmah

Spiritual Experience:
Vision of Harmony and God

Life Path Keynote:
Power of Angels and Guiding Spirits

Primary Symbols:

Hebrew Letter:	Heh (window)
Astrological Influence:	Aries
Tarot Designation:	Emperor (sometimes the Star)
Colors:	Scarlet
Magical Gifts:	Spear; all solar symbols; hawk; chalice

Pathworking Benefits:
Renewed life; visions of the Divine; devotion to the Great Work; spirit contact; greater initiative; strengthens connections to others

Strengths Achieved:
Visionary energies; revelation of life potentials; courage; ability to inspire; attunement to higher orders

Weaknesses Revealed:
Disrespect for authority; bitterness; unclear focus; disassociation from people; egotism; foolhardiness; acting without forethought

14th Path – Binah to Chokmah

Spiritual Experience:
Vision of Divine Sorrow

Life Path Keynote:
Illumination, Fertility and Creative Power

Primary Symbols:

Hebrew Letter:	Daleth (door)
Astrological Influence:	Venus
Tarot Designation:	Empress
Colors:	Emerald Green
Magical Gifts:	Full moon; equal armed cross; egg; dove

Pathworking Benefits:
Fertility; illumination of potentials; revelation of the hidden; devotion; birth; love and sharing; belief in the impossible

Strengths Achieved:
Knowledge of birth; merging of imagination and reality; attractiveness; understanding of the feminine; joy, love and reproduction

Weaknesses Revealed:
Disbelief; failure to merge creative principles for prosperity; feeling unattractive; lack of femininity; lack of joy; inappreciative

13th Path - Tiphareth to Kether

Spiritual Experience:
Vision of Harmony through Union with God

Life Path Keynote:
Glory of the Dark Night of the Soul

Primary Symbols:

Hebrew Letter:	Gimel	(camel)
Astrological Influence:	Moon	
Tarot Designation:	High Priestess	
Colors:	Blue	
Magical Gifts:	Moon; bow and arrow; silver; the dog	

Pathworking Benefits:
True knowledge; completion of work; true power of faith in the Divine; peace with oneself; giving birth to the Light within

Strengths Achieved:
Faith; removal of barriers between worlds; resourcefulness; self-reliance; wealth of intuition; revelation of hidden

Weaknesses Revealed:
Self-made obstacles; unbalanced emotions; inability to see purpose; overdependence; conflict of being alone with being lonely; unreliance

12ᵗʰ Path - Binah to Kether

Spiritual Experience:
Vision of Movement from Sorrow to Divine Union

Life Path Keynote:
Hopes, Visions and True Magick

Primary Symbols:

Hebrew Letter:	Beth	(house)
Astrological Influence:	Mercury	
Tarot Designation:	Magician	
Colors:	Yellow	
Magical Gifts:	Caduceus; Ibis; sword, cup, wand and pentacle; all seeing eye	

Pathworking Benefits:
Realization of our abilities; alchemy and magick; true vision of the spiritual; strong emotions; artistic and creative endeavors

Strengths Achieved:
Nourishment; wisdom and dexterity in life; seership; balance of intuition and rational; intelligence

Weaknesses Revealed:
Failure to recognize ability; blocked vision; restlessness; unbalanced emotions; unwilling to take advantage of growth situations

11th Path - Chokmah to Kether

Spiritual Experience:
Vision of Union with God

Life Path Keynote:
Simplicity and Becoming Again as a Child

Primary Symbols:

Hebrew Letter:	Aleph (ox)
Astrological Influence:	Air
Tarot Designation:	The Fool
Colors: (sunshine)	Bright Pale Yellow
Magical Gifts:	Fan; hat with one feather; staff and a rose

Pathworking Benefits:
Simplification of life; completion of work; initiation of new endeavors; stimulation of intuition and artistic abilities; prophecy

Strengths Achieved:
Innocence and trust; mental clarity; cooperation; poise in the universe; wisdom teachings

Weaknesses Revealed:
Over complications; fog like perspective; repetitive; hyperactivity; coldness; distrust

Chapter Seven

Your Personal Life Path

Pathworking is a dynamic method of undertaking and accelerating our personal spiritual quest. Qabalistic pathworking clears the bridges between the different levels of consciousness represented on the Tree of Life, giving us access to any level of consciousness at any time to any degree we desire. It is a powerful tool for those who wish truly to be the creators and heroes of their own life journey. Through Qabalistic pathworking we become the mythic hero in our individual spiritual journeys. We write and star in our own heroic tale.

Hero tales provide pictures of the journey we each must take if we wish to open to higher initiations, mysteries and energies of the universe. Almost every major myth or heroic tale starts with a younger individual leaving home to seek a fortune in any of a multitude of forms. These tales often have older characters who, when met along the road, offer advice and assistance. These elders represent those who work as mediators between the physical and spiritual worlds and who become available (showing up in our life) as we expand our awareness and open to new possibilities. In the ancient tales and myths, it is how the advice is acted upon that determines the future of the young seeker and how progress is made.

One of the common forms of the hero's quest is the entering into service of a mighty king or queen, symbolic of a greater force - or even our own higher self. For many the call of the quest in tales and legends (and in real life) is a call to adventure and excitement, but it is not always recognized for what it truly is: *a time of growth and emergence into responsibility and maturity!*

It is a time of transition and a time of dynamic growth - growth that can entail some very strong emotional highs and some very intense emotional lows. It is a time of serious self-assessment (sometimes forced). The individual must examine the circumstances, people, situations and beliefs of his or her life. The individual must examine what has been lost, stolen, broken and/or no longer necessary, so that it can be cleaned out once and for all. This makes room within the hero's life for that which is more beneficial. It is a time for cleaning the attic.

Many enter into metaphysical and occult practices as a means of escaping their daily lives. They look for these mystical practices to solve their problems. Many see the spiritual path as leading up into some blinding light into which all of their troubles and problems will be dissolved. In reality metaphysical and mystical practices are paths to find the light within so that we can shine it out into our lives. If an individual has difficulty handling the situations daily life, invoking spiritual energies will not necessarily make things easier.

More likely, the spiritual energies will serve to intensify the daily, mundane circumstances of life - forcing a reconciliation or resolution of daily troubles and problems. Our own fears, doubts, limitations and perspectives - whether self created or imposed upon us by society - create barriers to accessing and expressing all of our highest capacities. Qabalistic pathworking shows us not only what our barriers are but where they are as well. It brings them to the surface so that we must do something about them. This forces a reckoning that ultimately makes us more responsible and stronger. At the same time it manifests other wonderful rewards for us.

When we start our journeys, everything may be goodness and light which is as it should be. This is the strengthening process, preparing us for greater tasks and mysteries to be undertaken. When we use pathworking, we are proclaiming to the universe: *"I am ready to take on greater work and responsibility, and I am taking it on in full awareness of what that entails!'* This is why learning about your own personal Qabalistic path and undertaking it first is often the first empowering step to your own higher initiation.

Pathworking and Initiation

Pathworking accelerates the meeting of karma and it accelerates the release of our higher gifts. This makes it easier to manifest them into our daily lives. Instead of seeking some light to shine down upon us, through pathworking we develop our own light to shine out from us.

The paths are bridges that link the various sephiroth on the Tree of Life. These bridges between the various levels of our consciousness become congested with outworn ideas, attitudes and perceptions. They become clogged with our fears, our doubts and a multitude of hindrances that we accumulate throughout life. Pathworking is a means of clearing the bridges. It is comparable to clearing out clogged water lines. Doing so enables the water to run more freely and more powerfully throughout our house.

When we tap the specific sephiroth, as we learned to do in parts one and two, the result is *ILLUMINATION*. Illumination is a higher form of consciousness which changes the mind, enhancing all of our perceptions. When we begin to bridge more strongly the different levels for even greater growth through pathworking, we institute *INITIATION*. We open ourselves to the Mysteries of Life.

All work with the Qabala sets energy in motion that will play itself out within our daily lives - through the people and situations that are in it. This is why working with the Tree of Life demands continual watchfulness. Nothing is insignificant and what we experience may be manifesting due to our work with a particular Qabalistic exercise. We must realize that everything in life can have a hidden message and lesson within it (if we choose to see it), and that it may be related specifically to a particular exercise that we performed.

The Mysteries on the Tree

The bottom four sephiroth (Malkuth, Yesod, Hod and Netzach) and their corresponding paths comprise what are called THE *LESSER MYSTERIES*. They activate energies for the unfoldment and the development of the personality. They are linked to forces that involve searching for and awakening more than just a physical existence. Through these paths and sephiroth, the seeker learns to look beyond. The tests activated by these paths involve the development of good character, which form the foundation of higher development. They also involve learning to open and access the subconscious more easily.

Everything associated with the Lesser Mysteries involves other people and our relationships with them. Our greatest learning comes through the groups we encounter, formally and otherwise. The Lesser Mysteries involve learning to maintain a sound mind and body, to control instincts and passions, and to strengthen the mind.

THE GREATER MYSTERIES involve the middle three sephiroth (Tiphareth, Geburah and Chesed) and their corresponding paths. These mysteries involve learning to awaken and develop individuality - those unique creative energies and abilities that last more than a single lifetime. These are the qualities that we strengthen and manifest more each lifetime. Within the Greater Mysteries is the lesson of true faith which opens the veils to true spiritual insight. The lessons at these levels change our focus from the outer world to the inner world. Through these levels,

Mysteries on the Tree of Life

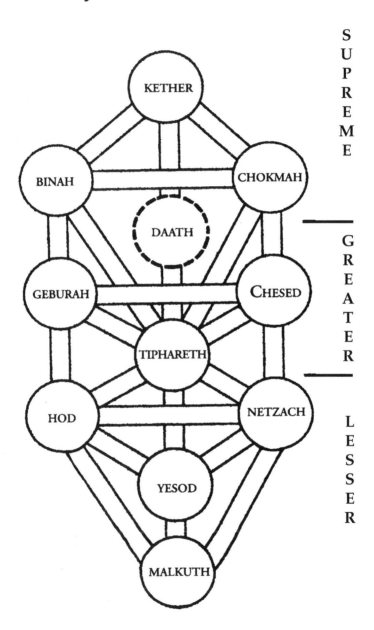

S
U
P
R
E
M
E

G
R
E
A
T
E
R

L
E
S
S
E
R

our inner principles are focused and dedicated to higher service.

The Greater Mysteries always involve probationary periods in which our dedication to the higher is tested. It is when working with these that we meet what many occultists refer to as *the inner plane adept* - who will guide us in greater teachings and the development of dedication.

Dedication, however, does not imply neglect of the physical for the spiritual because it is only by our work in the physical that we learn to apply our lessons. Dedication involves recognizing that some duties in the physical will have precedence over work in the mysteries. It is here that we learn that the fulfillment of our daily obligations to ourselves and to others demonstrates our dedication to the higher and that our ability to fulfill these obligations creatively and positively may be part of our probationary testing. And sometimes this means we must put aside specific, personal metaphysical studies in order to fulfill our obligations.

Through the sephiroth and paths of the Greater Mysteries, we learn to act upon our own resources, without reliance on others. The personality is sacrificed for the spiritual. This involves facing debts and duties within our life and learning to take responsibility for our thoughts, feelings and actions. It involves learning to be alone without being lonely. It requires learning to consciously work out our individual destiny.

THE SUPREME MYSTERIES are those that deal more specifically with teaching us the path of our true spiritual essence, its effects upon our physical life and the understanding of how spiritual life and energy is structured. These mysteries involve the upper three sephiroth (Binah, Chokmah and Kether), along with their corresponding paths.

The energies of the Supreme Mysteries often play themselves out in our lives more abstractly. Many times they involve great leaps of faith. It is through them that we begin to understand how everything works together, and we learn to set it in motion for the benefit of all - not just for ourselves. We begin to recognize and understand the universal rhythms and how to align ourselves with them.

All of the mysteries and lessons associated with the sephiroth and the paths are of equal importance in our lives and our evolution. They simply serve different functions. They are simply different expressions of energy to help us.

We work on all of these levels simultaneously, and most people are not even aware that the experiences within their lives are reflections of these mysteries. Through work with the Qabala and especially through pathworking, we attempt to become more cognizant of these energies and to more consciously control and direct it. We learn to be active within our life, stimulating and setting the energies in motion around us consciously rather than being passive and letting the universe play upon us. By learning to set the energies in motion, we accelerate our teaching and our learning. We learn to control them without being overcome by them.

Discovering the Personal Life Path

Almost all of the esoteric sciences can be applied to the Qabala. Numerology - the mysticism of numbers - is no exception. Archetypal energies are reflected in many forms. They are reflected through symbols and images, colors, sounds and even numbers. All energy and life is vibration, and numbers are the mathematical correlation of those vibrations in relation to us or to any aspect of life.

Numerology is an ancient science that dates back almost 10,000 years BC. The masters of the fourth root race (Atlantean Epoch) recognized that everything in nature was geometrically formed. All of the world's scriptures - such as the Vedas, the Zohar, the Torah, the Bible and others - cannot be understood in their most esoteric sense without an understanding of vibration and the significance of numbers.

The masters of Israel were well versed in the Law of Vibration and how archetypal forces were reflected through it. The 22 letters of the Hebrew alphabet were considered the 22 steps the soul had to take to mastership and as the 22 paths that bridged and united all the levels of our consciousness. Each letter and its numerical correspondence indicates an initiation - a path we must walk to develop mastership.

We each come into life to learn certain lessons and develop certain capacities, and we bring natural abilities to assist us in our life path. Because of the density of physical life, we often lose contact with the soul and its purpose for this incarnation. In its wisdom though, the soul chooses a time, a date, a place, and a name - all with numerical and archetypal correspondences. They play upon us subtly and unconsciously, creating situations in which we undergo lessons we have chosen. We are not controlled by these influences, but becoming aware of them can increase our understanding of what we hoped to accomplish in this lifetime. They can help us understand why we have appeared on this planet at this time, what lessons we have to learn and how to use our innate tools to assist us in overcoming obstacles.

Our name is one of our key energy signatures and can reveal much about our potentials. This has been the subject of two previous works - *THE SACRED POWER IN YOUR NAME* and *THE MAGICKAL NAME.* Although there are applications of our name to the Tree of Life, we will not be examining such within this text.

Our primary focus will be on our birth date and how it reflects the energy of our path in life. We will use some basic numerology techniques with our birth date, to determine two things:

1. The particular path on the Tree of Life that reflects the path we have chosen to walk and learn from most strongly within this particular incarnation and

2. The particular sephira or level of consciousness that we can draw upon most strongly to help us in our life path.

Our Birth Date on the Tree of Life

Our birth date can be translated into numbers which can be correlated to the Tree of Life. It can be a link to a particular sephira and a particular tarot card, thereby indicating a specific path for us. In other words, if we know which tarot card our birth date relates to, we can discern which of the paths on the Tree of Life we have come to work with more strongly. This in turn helps us to put into perspective many of our past life experiences.

Our birth date is a dominant energy signature. It reflects the keynote of our existence. When applied to the Qabala, it can reveal which level on the Tree of Life can be used more easily to realize our true happiness and success. It can also indicate exactly which path - with all of its tests, initiations and rewards - we must walk to achieve mastership in this lifetime.

Our birth date corresponds to our life path - our destiny. In traditional numerology, this is the school of life lesson, what we have come to learn in this lifetime. It reflects the lessons that the soul wants to complete here on Earth, along with the path of experience necessary for our further development. It indicates the path we walk, the strengths and weaknesses we are more likely to encounter, the archetypal symbols and images most effective for us and what we are ultimately striving for.

The birth date, when translated to the Tree of Life, provides three powerful keys to our unfoldment. It will tell us the sephira, that level of our consciousness which can most easily reveal and illumine aspects of our life more fully. Through this sephira we can discover the archangel who will often serve as a predominant teacher and source for our illumination upon the spiritual path. It will tell us a major planetary influence for our life. The divine name associated with the sephira will serve often as a protecting influence and call for guidance, when chanted and meditated upon.

The second key involves translating the birth date to a specific path to determine where and how our tests and initiations are more likely to occur. This requires translating the birth date into a corresponding tarot trump, which then determines our life path. The tarot trump also serves as a bridge to the archetypal forces of that path. The divine names and archangels associated with the sephiroth being bridged will help us in our endeavors, guiding and protecting us while pursuing our path throughout our life.

A third but less specific key involves the path associated with your astrological sign. An old axiom states: "As above, so below." Within us is a specific reflection of the universe with its stellar and planetary influences. Those

TheTree and the Hebrew Alphabet

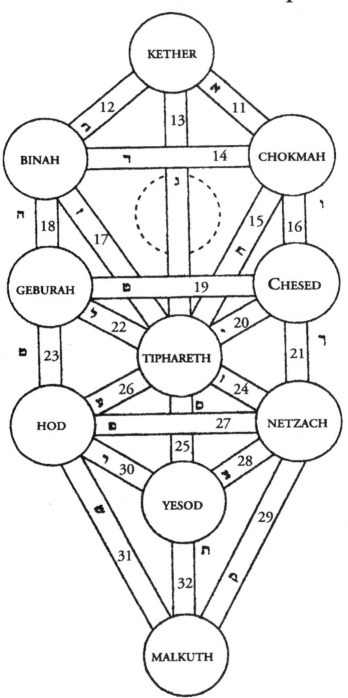

general stellar patterns are defined and explained through the science of astrology. The path, associated with our astrological sign, provide clues to a basic, universal soul plan that we have come into this life to work upon. It is not as specific as the personal sephira and our birth path, but it will provide clues to innate gifts we have chosen to develop and lessons we have chosen to undertake.

How to Figure the Correspondences

1. Converting the Birth date to Numbers

To discover the specific sephira and the specific path, we must reduce the birth date to numbers. The digits are then added individually. From this, they are reduced in two fashions to help us determine our personal sephira and life path.

Begin with the month in which you were born. Use the number for the month rather than the name. For example: January = 1, February = 2, March = 3, etc. Add to this the day and the year. For the year use the complete designation - no abbreviations (i.e. 1962 rather than '62).

04 04 1949
8   23 = 13

SAMPLE:
March 1, 1960   = 3-1-1960   = 3+1+1+9+6+0   = 20

When the total is achieved, we will reduce it in two ways to determine the individual sephira and the specific life path.

2. Determining Your Sephira from the Birth

There are only ten sephira upon the Tree of Life, each with its corresponding number:

1/10	Kether
2	Chokmah
3	Binah
4	Chesed
5	Geburah
6	Tiphareth
7	Netzach
8	Hod
9	Yesod
10/1	Malkuth

(Note that for both Malkuth and Kether, the numbers 1 and 10 both apply. Those whose birthdates reduces to 1 or 10 should work with both levels. Both Kether and Malkuth will be important in the life of these individuals.)

In our sample in step one, the birth date of March 1, 1960 numerically becomes 20. This number must be reduced to become 10 or less. Thus the 20 becomes 2+0 which equals 2.

SAMPLE:
   March 1, 1960 = 3+1+1+9+6+0 = 20 = 2+0 =
                   2 = Chokmah

In this sample, the number 2 represents the sephira which the individual has come to awaken and use throughout his or her life for greater illumination. And as we can see from the chart, the number two applies to the sephira of Chokmah. It is through the second sephira or Chokmah that the individual will find the archangelic and angels teachers most influential. It is through this level that assimilation and understanding of the individual's life experiences will occur most strongly. Reading and meditating more about our particular and individual sephira will yield much more insight into our life experiences.

3. Determining the Life Path from our Birth date

To determine the specific life path on the Tree of Life, our birth date must be correlated to a tarot card. Although there are 22 paths, the numbering of the actual paths begins with 11. For this reason, we do not apply the birth date number directly to the path number. For example, with the birth date we have used above (March 1, 1960), we cannot apply the number 2 to a specific path because the paths actually begin with the number 11.

NOTE:
Do not apply the birth date number directly to a path number. It must first be applied to a tarot trump, from which we determine the actual path our birth date relates to!

The birth date must be related to a tarot trump in order to determine the specific life path on the Tree of Life. The tarot trump comprises 22 cards total (corresponding to the 22 letters in the Hebrew alphabet). The tarot trump, like the Hebrew letters, are associated with specific paths, thus by linking our birth date to a tarot card, we can determine our specific life path.

Birth Date and Your Life Path

Birth #	Tarot Trump	Corresponding Life Path
1	Magician	Binah to Kether (12th Path)
2	High Priestess	Tiphareth to Kether (13th Path)
3	Empress	Binah to Chokmah (14th Path)
4	Emperor	Tiphareth to Chokmah (15th Path)
5	Hierophant	Chesed to Chokmah (16th Path)
6	Lovers	Tiphareth to Binah (17th Path)
7	Chariot	Geburah to Binah (18th Path)
8	Strength	Geburah to Chesed (19th Path)
9	Hermit	Tiphareth to Chesed (20th Path)
10	Wheel of Fortune	Netzach to Chesed (21st Path)
11	Justice	Tiphareth to Geburah (22nd Path)
12	Hanged Man	Hod to Geburah (23rd Path)
13	Death	Netzach to Tiphareth (24th Path)
14	Temperance	Yesod to Tiphareth (25th Path)
15	Devil	Hod to Tiphareth (26th Path)
16	Tower	Hod to Netzach (27th Path)
17	Star	Yesod to Netzach (28th Path)
18	Moon	Malkuth to Netzach (29th Path)
19	Sun	Yesod to Hod (30th Path)
20	Judgment	Malkuth to Hod (31st Path)
21	World	Malkuth to Yesod (32nd Path)
22	Fool	Chokmah to Kether (11th Path)

We begin as we did before, by translating our birth date into numbers. In determining the personal sephira, we kept reducing the number until it was 10 or less because there are ten sephiroth on the Tree of Life. In determining our personal life path, we reduce only until the birth date number is **22 or less** because there are 22 tarot trumps, each corresponding to one of the 22 paths of wisdom.

SAMPLE:
March 1, 1960 = 3+1+1+9+6+0 = 20 =
The Judgment Card
Judgment Card = Path of Malkuth to Hod (31st Path)

By using the table on the previous page, we can determine which tarot card applies to our birth date. From that tarot card, we can determine the path we have come to truly work with. By examining that path we can discern which energies will play upon us more strongly throughout our life. We can explore more fully the path our soul has chosen to walk towards mastership in this lifetime.

The magical techniques, pathworkings and meditations on that path will reveal much insight into our life experiences. It can even reveal how close or far off we are from our soul's original intentions. Work with this life path can also reveal to us how best to get our lives back on track.(Keep in mind though that we always have free will, and even though we may have chosen a particular path prior to our incarnation, we do not have to hold to it. It can be more difficult when we change our course though, and it can explain many of the circumstances we have experienced.)

One other method that can reveal further insights into our soul's potentials and tasks is by examining the path associated with our astrological sign. It is not as specific as the path of the actual birth date, but its energies will also be reflected within our life to some degree.

Remember that we use the Qabala - the sephiroth and the paths of wisdom - to expand our awareness of who we are and what we can do. We use it for revelation and transformation. Connecting them all, finding and exploring all of the various correspondences, will provide much to assist us in our own great alchemical changes in life.

Pathworking Exercise

Creating the Life Adventure

Benefits:

- awakens us to our life path
- stimulates resolution of problems
- awakens you to your potentials
- opens to new possibilities
- brings awareness of our life quest

We can learn to perform the pathworking in a much more personalized, ritualistic manner. In many ways, this is like role playing a tale or myth - acting it out, only we are creating the storyline ourselves. This form of pathworking takes the energy that we set in motion with the pathworking and releases it into our daily lives very dynamically. It will powerfully reveal in the weeks that follow what your true desire and life purpose is.

This is a bit more advanced pathworking. But it is one of the most important that we can do. Although it requires a familiarity with the path and its basic qualities, it is still very beneficial to uncovering issues and unfolding greater potentials. Since it is a more personal pathworking though - related intimately to you, be aware that the effects will be stronger.

To accomplish this life adventure pathworking, we begin by contemplating and deciding what we wish to accomplish through the pathworking. If working with a journel, give this more creative working a title, just as if you were titling a short story. In essence, we are translating our purpose into a dramatic or story scenario. We will empower it with the appropriate symbols, and then play it out in both the mind and act it out physically aswell - just as you acted adventures out as a kid.

Putting the purpose into dramatic form, to act it out, is extremely powerful. It gives your purpose structure and animation through the imagery that you create. The ancients used such ceremonies, mystery plays and rituals to stimulate energies and to resolve problems. Theater was an important part of the ancient mystery schools. The symbolic enactment of universal energies brought about a dynamic release of them within the participant's physical lives. This has been a form of sympathetic magic used throughout the world.

Trust your own intuition in creating the pathworking scenario, but you must employ the basic symbology of the path. The symbols serve as the catalysts, and without them our efforts will be impotent. Consciousness is awareness joined with the appropriate action.

1. Choose the area of your life that you wish to impact.

2. Study your life path and reflect on how that path will likely impact what it is that you wish.

3. Review the path and even make notes about it in your journal.

Make note of the purpose for this working, and why you have chosen to perform this with the designated path.

4. Create and play through a scenario in your mind.

Determine the ideal manner you would like to see the energies manifest. If the pathworking is to resolve a problem, visualize you meeting it, facing it and resolving it. If it is to accomplish a goal or achieve something, visualize the easiest and best way this could unfold for you.

Use the ancient tales and myths as a guideline. See yourself upon a quest, searching out gold or something valuable that represents your goal for the pathworking. If the purpose is to overcome something within your life or to move past an obstacle, make that obstacle mythical in proportions. Some visualize their obstacles as monsters that must be slain, etc. Use your own creative imagination!

When we use this particular technique, we are trying to release energy into our life that has been blocked or hindered, so that we have full access to our resources at any time. This activation intensifies situations to the point where they can no longer be ignored. We are forcing resolution so our energies are free to pursue more creative and productive endeavors. The gift is sometimes hidden within the problem, so that only by facing what is hindering us, can the gift be released.

4. Use the symbols of the path in the scenario.

Make sure that you use the appropriate colors, fragrances, Hebrew letter, etc. within your pathworking. These may be a part of the scenery or even the dress of the individuals you incorporate into your pathworking. You decide. Part of what you are learning to do is to use your creative imagination in order to manifest conditions that will benefit your life.

5. Enter the Tree of Life.

Bring to life the temple as we learned earlier. Once the temple has been called forth, visualize a door in the back of the temple. Imagine symbols of the path engraved into the door. Then open the door and walk through the doorway into the path and your adventure.

6. Walk the path, allowing the drama to unfold.

It is a good idea to work into your adventure some assistance from someone else. I personally like to have the archangel show up to provide guidance, strength or general assistance in my scenarios. It also serves as extra protection.

Make sure you encounter the symbols of the path about halfway through as always. This is powerful to act out in the outdoors.

I like to do it among lots of trees, choosing two to represent the two sephira. And then I play out the scenario I created, incorporating the symbols and images of the path as I move slowly from one tree or temple to the second in the distance.

Althoug initially you may do this only in your mind in a meditative fashion. In time though - when you are truly ready for powerful results - you may want to enact this scenario. It is a type of magickal role-playing, but not of the dungeons and dragons variety. In an earlier work, *MAGICKAL DANCE*, I described a variety of ways in which dance and theater can be used ceremonially. I discuss this a little in part four, but it is one of the most powerful tools for activating dynamic archetypal forces to play within our lives.

7. Enter into the second temple.
As the drama concludes and your purpose is accomplished, create a doorway into the second temple and bring it to life. There allow the two archangels to comment and clarify your experiences and what you may expect to unfold in the days ahead as a result of it.

8. Close the temples and exit the Tree of Life, bringing your gifts out with you.

9. Ground the energies and record impressions within your journal.

10. Special reminders.
We have created a scenario according to our own unique purpose. Visualizing it being enacted is the same as daydreaming. The only difference is that now we are empowering the energies with specific symbols and then

we are grounding the energies. We chose specific images and clusters of images, placing them within a scenario that reflected our personal purpose. We then linked them to archetypal forces.

With this kind of pathworking we are recommitting powerfully to our spiritual goals. This implies that we must transmute what we are now to create something greater. Resolution of present situations brings change, and change brings growth.

If conflicts and imbalances arise or intensify, it is only so we will be forced to look at new possibilities. We are resolving our life experiences by consciously working from the outer to the inner and back to the outer again. We are bridging and expanding our resources. We are learning to weave together the elements of our physical life with our spiritual life. Rather than remaining passive creatures, we are becoming conscious *creators* of our own life experiences!

Astrological Correspondences to the Tree

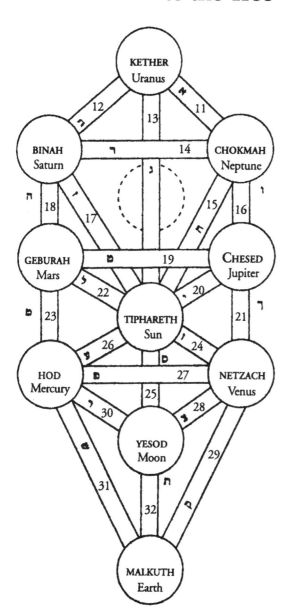

32 Saturn
31 Primal Fire
30 Sun
29 Pisces
28 Aquarius
27 Mars
26 Capricorn
25 Sagittarius
24 Scorpio
23 Primal Water
22 Libra
21 Jupiter
20 Virgo
19 Leo
18 Cancer
17 Gemini
16 Taurus
15 Aries
14 Venus
13 Moon
12 Mercury
11 Air

Using Qabalistic Paths

There are many ways of using these three bits (your personal sephira, your personal path and your astrological path) of information for tremendous enlightenment and benefit, and you will discover new ways of doing so. One such way is by using the paths for insight and help in personal relationships.

The Tree of Life can be map to show best ways of working with the other person to find greater things - good and bad - in common. By examining where you both fall on the tree of life, you can look for common sephira or paths that will help you find something in common.

Let's say for example, that you are a Cancer (path of Geburah to Binah) and someone else in your life is a Gemini (path of Tiphareth to Binah), focusing upon things associated with Binah (a primal source of Mother energy, including Mother Nature) will draw the two together.

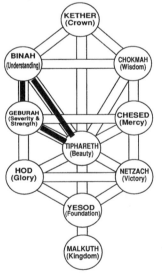

Don't be afraid to explore. Draw out the connections on the Tree and examine the possibilities and relationships.

This couple may choose to work on the path from Tiphareth to Geburah, creating a triangle of strength. This path is one that both need to make the relationship better and more compatible, especially in these two signs that are

160

To Strengthen Relationships

so often romantically incompatible from an astrological perspective.

The same can be done with the personal life paths. By compariing them and looking for commonalities, the relationship can be stronger. For married couples, take the wedding date and find the life path associated with it and compare it to the two personal life paths of the individual.

So for example, Let's say that one person has a personal life 3 = Empress = path of Binah to Chokmah and the other has a personal life number of 1 = Magician = path of Binah to Kether. In addition they have a marriage life number of 9 = Hermit =path of Tiphareth to Chesed.

The path of Binah to Tiphareth may be essential for both to work on to connect their personal life paths with their marriage life path and faciliate the marriage. In this example, Binah is common to both and so working the path

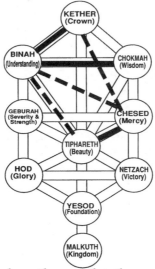

from Binah to Tiphareth may be the easiest way to make the marriage path more compatible for both. Or the couple may use the two hidden paths and create a dynamic pyramid of power in the relationship.

Part IV -

The Secret
of
Dancing the Tree

Chapter Eight

The Secret of Dancing the Tree

Working with the Qabalistic Tree of Life is a creative process. That is why sound, music and dance must be an essential part of it. Music and dance make us more alive and touch us on other levels than just the physical. They form a bridge between heaven and Earth that we can all learn to use within our day-to-day lives.

Dance is preeminent in ancient ritual and ceremony. It was used to awaken and stir the forces and energies of life and magic. It was, and still is, a way to link the mental realms with the physical. It can be used to transport the dancer from the physical reality to more ethereal ones – from the profane to the sacred. It is a metaphor of life and the process of manifestation. Thought creates within the mental world, leading to actions in the physical. We think and then we act.

The purpose of any physical ritual behavior is to direct and focus the consciousness. Our physical beings have a unique capacity for blocking our evolutionary process. Directed physical behavior, such as dance, can overcome this tendency, and help us to align our physical responses with our spiritual goals. It enables our physical energies to hold contact with our higher forces.

Dance fuses the hemispheres of the brain, linking right and left - the intuitive with the rational. Through dance movements and gestures, the essence of music is absorbed into the physical and then experienced on subtler levels. The central nervous system and the neuro-muscular systems transform the musical rhythms into a movement pattern. We become driven by it and are led away from the familiar focus of the everyday world. In the past, individuals would surrender to and be possessed by it; today it is important that we enter in full consciousness and actually learn to ride the rhythms to the inner world, with our wills intact.

Isadora Duncan evolved a theory of the physiological process of dance. She insisted that movement and breathing are inseparable. And to the ancients, life was breath. All movement is carried aloft and then returned to Earth through inhalation and exhalation. The movements change the breathing, and thus change the bridges to other levels of consciousness. To take it a step further, by aligning physical movements consciously, we can reach newer and deeper levels of consciousness.

Sacred Dance and Movement

The purpose of ritual dance is to make the world of energies and powers physical. We attempt to re-express these energies upon the physical plane, so that as unique individuals we learn to utilize them in the manner most suitable for us.

All dance is gesture, and we each have gestures that are uniquely our own. They give us color and enhancement. Gesture is related to the human condition in its creation of a desired appearance without truly representing it. Gestures serve to link the outer man with the inner, and to bridge us to our divine selves.

The modern concepts of dance for the average individual have changed dramatically over the centuries. Dance was part of the ancient mysteries, and its substance was the realm of magic, enchantment and ancient powers which lived within caves, forests and all of creation. It was the sacred instrument of worship, prayer and true magic, whether utilized within temple worship or in the invoking of rain.

The role of magic within dance has been diminished by our modern, materialistic thought processes. Actual energies are created or awakened in all forms of dance, even in modern social dances. In these, magnetic energies are stimulated, but we have moved to touching romantic realms rather than the sacred realms.

The ancients recognized the possibility of such changes and so stressed continual watchfulness and control over the dance energies. They recognized the therapeutic and educational value of dance, but they focused upon its sacred aspect because they knew that all movement invoked very subtle and powerful energies. They recognized that the male and female participants were not just dancers, but priests and priestesses. As such, there was a need for greater awareness and control of these energies.

Sacred dance was a means of transcending our humanity. The dancer could gain control over normally automatic responses by evoking emotions and energies and then channeling them through the dance. In this manner, transcendence over these lower energies could be achieved. Sacred dance was an art that could fire man's vitality and revive depleted energies. It involved improvisation and individual creativity. Every movement and gesture was linked to the purpose of the dance.

All human activity is a kind of dance and ritual, but it is time to re-tap the ancient approaches to dance ritual. Non-believers will have little understanding of the true ritual power of dance. For many the techniques will simply be a form of spiritual window-shopping. The dervishes will only be dancers. The Catholic mass becomes little more than a spectacle. These individuals must be reminded that religious ritual of any kind is not -nor should it ever be- performed for its own sake. (This may, in fact, be the primary problem of the weekly mass.) It should be performed as a way of reaching another level of being, as a way of releasing spiritual meaning into our lives. Ritual is not meant to be performed for audiences, which can be a profaning in many ways. And to simply adopt the outer appearances of ritual is to start the process of death.

True sacred dance is very ancient. It is the outer expression of the inner spirit. The modem process of dancing the Tree of Life is not to just re-enact ancient mysteries. Our energies have changed too much for it to be effective or useful. We are also somewhat disassociated with much of the true esoteric teachings of the ancients. We must become priests and priestesses of New Age dance. That requires us to remember that energies are *not* created by the dance but simply invoked and challenged by it. It also requires that we remember that the energies invoked function less through our talent for dancing than through our participation! It enhances the ability to envision a second world - the major source of our esoteric knowledge.

*"Just as he
who dances
in the body...acquires the
right to share
in the round dance,
so he who dances in the spirit
acquires the right to dance
in the round of creation."
- St. Ambrose*

Dancing the Tree of Life

The Tree is an ancient symbol for the axis of the world. The entire world - heaven and Earth - spins upon it. Dancing the Tree of Life is a way of setting the world in motion. We have our roots in the Earth (the underworld), but like a tree, our branches can spread and reach heavenward. Dancing the Tree (climbing the tree) is equated with the passing from one plane of being to another. Traditionally, the Tree (like all gateways) is guarded by a dragon or monster which must be overcome before the treasure can be attained - before the fruit can be picked. Esoterically, this is the overcoming of our lower selves. This does not mean that we slay or kill the dragon. We must harness and control our dragons - our energies. They are a part of us while we are in the physical, but we can learn to control them and redirect their energies in a creative manner to enhance our lives.

This is where the power of dance in ritual finds its greatest creativity. The sacred dance provides a means for confronting and harnessing our dragon energies for creative expression within our lives. This is the key to the great alchemical change. It is not the killing of negative energies. It is the transmutation of them within our lives!

Basic Dynamics

Most recently in our history, we find religious dancing taking place within churches and temples; but many earlier groups created temples by marking off sacred circles for the dance on the Earth itself. One common theme was the imitation of angels dancing in heavenly rings about the throne of God. This led to many of the circle dances which will be discussed later within this chapter, which create a resonance, or sympathetic vibration (harmony), within the participants.

Sacred dance helps us to transcend humanity. It is this aspect that has been neglected for centuries and yet which we are all capable of reawakening. It is more than just a symbolic expression of an individual's personal beliefs. In many cases, such as in the ancient Kachina rites, the participants become sacred reflections of the powers of the universe. A basic premise behind all esoteric teaching is that we are the microcosm - a reflection of the macrocosm, or universe. We have all of the energies of the universe within us. Sacred dance was a means of stimulating them and bringing them out of the deeper levels of our consciousness.

At the root of most ceremonial use of dance was sympathetic magic. The movements and gestures create thoughtforms, vortices of energy, fusing thought and action. The ancients understood that dance, by its ability to invoke energy upon the physical plane, could shape the circumstances of nature simply by focusing that contagious quality of energy. It comes down to that ancient Hermetic Principle, "As above, so below; as below, so above." What we do on one level affects all other levels. The stronger we focus our energies and concentration, the stronger and greater will be the effect. This is what makes dance so powerful!

Religious or sacred dancing has been a functioning part of every society and civilization throughout the world. The shamans and priests used music and dance to induce a trance state. They utilized round or circle dances to imitate the path of the Sun. Chain dances were used to link the male and female energies, to bind both heaven and Earth, and to stimulate fertility. There were sword dances and thread-and-rope dances, as with the threads of Ariadne, the threads leading the dancer to the secret of knowledge throughout the maze of life. In all dances, intense feelings and the bodily movements were related.

In India the *devadasis* were the sacred dancing girls. They were married to the gods, and their dances represented the life of the gods they were married to. Egypt was a great dancing center. Its ancient dancers are even depicted within the hieroglyphics. The sacred mystery teachings were danced within the temples. The Nile and Cadiz were the greatest centers of ancient dancing. Cadiz was the sacred dancing school in Spain; it was also Egyptian in character. The Greek and the Roman mystery schools were strong in ritual dance. It formed - along with music - an essential part of their magickal and healing arts in the Orphic, Eleusinian and Bacchic mysteries. The snakelike winding of the Greek farandole dance of Provence symbolized the journey to the middle of the labyrinth - the pattern of the passage of the dead to the land of the afterlife. This was a common theme in many areas of the world. The dances were themes meant to stimulate multiple responses on a multitude of levels for the people.

The garments then, as they are today, were secondary to the movements. They can be discarded. Dances for higher states of consciousness are simple, personal and passionate. They do not and should not require great space. When a pattern is created or arranged for specific effects, it can create an illusion of great space, power and time. *Remember, we are fusing the mental and the physical.* It is not the talent but the participation that invokes the energy. The degree to which it is invoked is determined by the significance one can associate with the movements! Every gesture and movement is symbolic. The more meaning we attach to them, the deeper the level of consciousness and the greater the release of power.

Allow for individual expression. Do not necessarily allow the movements to become rote. Those movements and dances described within this book provide starting points. They are not the be-all and end-all for everyone. The process of evolvement requires that we assimilate, re-synthesize and adapt energies to what works for us as individuals. In essence, you are attempting to choreograph your own evolution, the awakening of your own unique energies. Yes, there are certain things that we can utilize and which serve as a foundation for us, but we must build from that point.

Postures of the Tree

There are physical movements and postures that not only correspond to the levels of the Qabalistic Tree of Life but also reflect those energies, drawing them down into our physical environments, where they express themselves into our lives. We can learn to use specific physical movements and postures to create a mind-set that enables easier access to the energies within the Tree of Life.

Many times the student of metaphysics has difficulty achieving results through meditative exercises and work. It seems they put in much time just trying to receive something. Working with the physical movements will deliver results much more quickly and effectively. When a person finally sits down to meditate, he or she may still have on their mind that last phone call, the argument with the boss, the trouble the kids were in all day, etc. These kinds of mundane energies can block access to the energies of the Tree of Life.

The physical movements enable the person to move in consciousness from the outer world and all of its hassles to the inner much more fluidly. It creates a mindset. The physical activity forces the mind to shift gears; it must then concentrate on the movements or gestures. The movements and postures described in this next section are not exercises and are not in any way meant to be looked upon as an exercise program. They are physical movements that help us to make that transition from the outer to the inner and back again fluidly and more easily.

Gestures, postures and movements express the inexpressible. They utilize both aspects of the brain, especially when we are aware of their significances. They are direct and potent ways of communicating with the deities that lie within us, and they aid us in concentration so that we can utilize our highest capacities. The more meaning we can ascribe to them, the more they become empowered.

The Eastern world has recognized this for ages. Fortunately, there is a growing integration of Eastern and Western philosophies and techniques. There are methods that we can apply specifically to Western forms of mysticism. The yoga movements and postures are simply outer expressions which represent inner degrees of consciousness. Yoga asanas are designed to be meditations in and of themselves, leading to greater depths. Using them in relation to the Western Qabalistic tradition reinforces the idea that there truly is nothing new under the Sun. There are simply different variations. All gods are aspects of the same god, and we each have a responsibility of finding the method or combination of methods which best awaken the divine within ourselves.

In yoga, *kriya* is a movement, asana, mudra or exercise to produce an altered state of consciousness. There is an outer kriya which involves asanas and mudras (postures and gestures) - basic physical expressions. And there is the inner aspect as well that was only reflected through the asanas. In dancing the Tree of Life, we are doing the same thing. We are learning to apply physical expressions to inner realities. We are utilizing physical exercises to awaken spiritual energies. This is the importance of the following asanas, as they can be applied to the Qabalistic Tree of Life. They are simple physical movements and positions that reflect inner levels of consciousness, while simultaneously releasing those inner latent energies and circulating them in a precise manner so that you can experience and utilize them to their fullest.

Postures are a language for communicating with the divinity that lies within us. Many of the yoga postures arose from a ritual mimicking of animals and nature to establish a magickal contact. We can use them in other ways to help us stimulate the energies on all levels within the Tree of Life. The postures activate and circulate the energies of the sephiroth in specific ways, all of which can be correlated to the levels of our consciousness. They are creating a form for the force to manifest. They serve as a bridge to energies of our self often hidden from us. They assist in our visualization, and they help us to release energy for the transformations we are seeking.

The positions and movements are kept simple throughout the rest of this part, but it must be understood that even more techniques and methods of Dancing the Tree exist. The positions described are firm but pleasant, and will develop a stable, healthy connection to the energy of the sephiroth and the paths, and enable us to attune to them more easily for their release within our physical life. The more difficult positions and movements for you (and they do vary from individual to individual) may indicate levels of consciousness that are more difficult for you to access and control. We can all do some variation, which means that we can at least access some aspect of the sephira or path and its energies within us. No aspect is entirely inaccessible. And the more we work with them, the easier they become and the more energy is released to us. Even our consciousness muscles need to be loosened up.

Specific movements and postures are described in the next chapter that activate the energies of each sephira - each level of our consciousness. By doing one of each, we can activate all of the energies of the Tree of Life for ourselves. We can also combine the movements of two sephira when we are performing a pathworking.

The postures can be done before and after any meditational work with that level of the Qabala. Doing it before will help open up that level of consciousness more fully. Doing it after the meditation will close the energy down and ground it into the physical. This can be done with any particular sephira or path by itself or with the entire Tree. Each must find the best way to work with them as individuals.

Balancing Pillars

Where do we begin with this? We begin and end always with simple balance. Whenever we work with any aspect of the Tree of Life, we want to do it while remaining balanced – physically, emotionally and mentally. The movements for balance are especially effective before and after meditation upon any level of the Tree. It enables a stable experiencing of the energies.

The right and left legs symbolize the right and left Pillars of the Tree of Life. We must learn to bring energy down into manifestation along each of the Pillars in a balanced manner. The postures help develop this ability. If we have more difficulty balancing on one leg than on the other, then the weaker leg will indicate that it is more difficult for you to balance the energies of the sephiroth associated with it as they apply to corresponding areas of your life:

Right Leg   = Pillar of Severity = Binah, Geburah & Hod
Left Leg   = Pillar of Mercy = Chokmah, Chesed &
                     Netzach
Both Legs   = Middle Pillar = Malkuth, Yesod, Tiphareth,
                     Kether (as well as Daath)

The first of these, as depicted on the following page, is the pose of the dancer. This is what we are becoming - the dancer of the Tree of Life. We are learning to choreograph our life and our resources for greater manifestation. In postures B and C, we are learning to balance the flow of energies down the Pillars of the Tree of Life represented by our legs. Many people have difficulty balancing upon one foot and leg. This is significant! Using again the Law of Correspondence, an inability to maintain balance in the physical would reflect an inability to balance the more subtle spiritual energies of the Tree of Life.

A.

This position enables you to awaken the energies of the Pillars so that you can become the Dancer in the Tree of Life.

B.

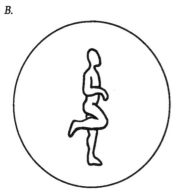

C.

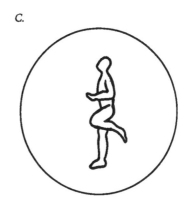

Postures which balance the Pillar energies of the Tree.

D.

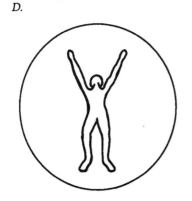

E.

Middle Pillar of Balance.

Grounding the energies of all three Pillars, before touching the specific sephiroth.

As we increase our ability to balance upon one leg, we increase our ability to balance our spiritual energies and consciousness as well. Most people find it easier to balance upon one leg than the other. This is also significant. It indicates the ability to balance the energies of one Pillar (and its levels of consciousness) more easily than the other. This then gives clues as to where we should concentrate some extra work. Remember that the Qabala will show us our greatest strengths and our greatest weaknesses, but we must be able to become cognizant of all aspects of our being and connect them. Again, as discussed earlier, this is a significant reason for working with pathworking.

In trying to discern which Pillar and its corresponding sephiroth are associated with which leg in the human body, one must see oneself as though backing into the Tree of Life diagram. The Middle Pillar becomes the spine. The left leg becomes the Pillar of Mercy, including Chokmah, Chesed and Netzach. The right leg then becomes the Pillar of Severity, including Binah, Geburah and Hod.

Postures D and E are for balancing and grounding the energies of the Middle Pillar and the two side Pillars. Position D brings all three Pillars into alignment and balance; position E grounds it all into the physical.

All of the balancing postures and movements train us in focusing our energies. They enable us to activate the flow of energy into our physical life in the most balanced manner possible. Many Hermeticists use similar postures in developing this kind of balance. Many practice assuming the post of the Hanged Man as depicted upon the tarot card. This in itself is appropriate, for the Hanged Man is hung upon the Tree of Life. Keeping the arms folded during all of these postures forces the individual to concentrate and work for even greater control. With the arms folded across the chest, we have a symbolic gesture of balance at the heart of our growth and evolution.

Creating a New Consciousness

Dancing is the gesture of the whole body. It allies the body and soul. It is the creation of the energy, not just the conscious awareness of it - although the latter is what leads to the former. It induces electrical changes in the body which induce specific states of awareness. We are using purposeful physical behavior to activate very real spiritual energies, so we must learn to dance with intention. Dancing raises the appropriate energies, aligns the physical with the corresponding spiritual, complements the intention and grounds the energy so we can more fully and easily experience it and then integrate it.

By more consciously using dance, we activate a very powerful force. We have discussed previously the hemispheres of the brain and the abilities that each possesses in its own right. Each hemisphere contains a force that we can learn to use. There is a third force that we have access to, and it is the force that is created when the other two are integrated. It is a force that is released from the heart and its very core. It goes beyond personal expression. It aligns our energies and rhythms with those of the cosmos. It aligns our soul with the cosmic soul. We become the true microcosm!

As we apply certain physical elements to spiritual concepts, and as we utilize physical postures and movements to enhance and invoke that which is beyond the physical, we are creating our own dance. We are creating a new world, a new consciousness and a new transformation.

Chapter Nine

Dancing the Sephiroth

Trees grow. Trees stretch and extend. They sway and shimmer with the wind. They dance. It is part of their existence. It should be no wonder then that dance is natural and empowering when applied to the Qabalistic Tree of Life. It becomes a moving prayer.

When we attach special significance to our movements, especially in delving into the universe and trying to touch more intimately the divine, we are *praying through bodily movement.*

It has been said that prayer is a state of heightened awareness and communication. Prayers can be simple or complicated; either way can work for us. Their style is dependent upon the import that we attach to them. When we pray the Tree of Life through movement, we are uniting all aspects of ourselves for the purpose of growth and enlightenment.

It is not the movement, but what we believe of the movement, that gives it power. Physical movement with intention is freeing and strengthening. It awakens our bodies to the spiritual while freeing the spiritual to nurture the body. Heaven and Earth. The roots and all the branches. We dance the Tree of Life every day, but our movements have no power. When we dance our prayers, we empower our lives. We climb the Tree to become nestled within its loving arms.

Dance and movement has been ignored in most modern mystical and magical practices and yet it is one of the most powerful means of activating power and opening ourselves to higher perceptions and greater potentials. To my knowledge, no book had ever applied dance and movement to the Qabala prior an earlier work of mine: *Imagick – the Magick of Images, Paths and Dance*. And yet it is still one of the most powerful and effective means of unveiling the hidden mysteries of the Tree of Life. And anyone who works with Qabala will benefit from it and achieve more by it.

Dancing Magic Circles

There are many ways of working out the dynamics of a dance that will open up the levels of consciousness that we know as the sephiroth in the Qabalistic Tree of Life. The fact that the sephiroth are depicted upon the Tree of Life as circles gives many clues to the use of circles for opening up those levels of consciousness to us. We can use dance and movement to awaken the Divine force that is most active within a particular sephira or level of consciousness. And one of the simplest and most effective ways is through the use of circle dancing.

The circle is a very powerful symbol and motion in both the physical and spiritual realms. It is a perfect symbol. It has no end and no beginning. We can start correctly anywhere within our evolutionary cycle. The movement in circles always brings to mind the turning of wheels (as in the wheel of life) and the movement of the Sun and planets. It is wholeness and the time cycles of the universe. It seals in and it seals out. The circle separates the inner from the outer. When moving in circular spirals, we can move from the outer into the inner realms or vice versa.

Making or dancing a circle is an act of creation. It is the marking off of sacred ground. When a circle dance is performed, the individual creates a sacred space within the mind (a place between the worlds, a point in which they intersect and play). The creation or marking off of a circle in Wiccan beliefs is sometimes referred to as "raising a cone of power." The circling creates a vortex of energy that is amplified by the combined wills of the participants.

The center of the circle is a point of focus. All dance - particularly circle dances - is a series of rhythmic steps around a central point, be it an altar, a fire, an individual or an idea. The dancing adds energy to the point within the circle - the *bindu*. The circle dance around the bindu creates a vortex of energy, while sealing out extraneous energies that could interfere with the ultimate purpose of the dance. By placing a symbol within the center and dancing around it, it can be protected. This also activates the energies of what is symbolized.

The circle dance is a sacred drama, employing physical motion to alter the mind and consciousness of the human being (audience or participant). It is a means to awaken deeper consciousness through physically enforced concentration. In the physical spiral motion, the individual is also mentally spiraling to other levels of consciousness.

Simple Sephira Circle Dance

Take time to meditate upon the sephira before the dance itself. Remember that you are a being with latent power within your consciousness. Visualize yourself as being part of the spiral dance since the beginning of time. You are participating - and have been - since time immemorial, whether conscious of it or not. Remember that every dance is actually two, an outer and an inner. The dance itself integrates these. And remember that dancing induces electrical changes within the human body, as it becomes saturated with the repetitive process of the steps.

Symmetry of steps is important and is powerfully effective, although it is not always necessary. As the circular movement unfolds, try a rhythm that is two steps forward and one step back. This particular movement is very effective for inducing an altered state of consciousness. It can even induce trance. (Forward - back, in - out, Heaven - Earth.) We shift the veils. We open secret doors.

As the steps of the dance unfold, there should be mental concentration upon the bringing inner energies into the outer world or vice versa. This is why steps should be simple. If the steps are too complicated, proper visualization of the effects will be limited. Visualizing the color of the sephira, accumulating and filling the circle while dancing the rotations, intensifies the effects.

Have a definite beginning and a definite end. A traditional beginning and end is the taking of three steps toward the center of the circle, bowing, and then proceeding with the dance. At the end, the individual or group takes three steps back from the center of the circle and bows.

There is often great question about which way to move, clockwise or counterclockwise. *Clockwise*, or deosil, movement activates the energy. It is masculine and solar in its effects. It has a centrifugal effect, pulling the energy from the inside to the outside. It draws from our spiritual to our physical for what we need. It stimulates power.

Counterclockwise, or widdershin, movement is inward or receptive in its energizing. It draws our outer consciousness into the inner. It activates the feminine and lunar energies. It can be used to awaken a greater sense of timelessness, opening the power of the past, present and future together. It draws energies from outside of us to us.

Hand movements are also important during the dancing of the circle. Hand movements and gestures have been known as the true universal language. To the ancient Hermeticists, *every action should have a specific* purpose *and significance.* All should be organized; every gesture should have its symbolic significance in alignment with the purpose of the dance. There should be no idleness of movement.

The hand in an upward (palms raised) position is a gesture of receptivity. The palm downward indicates more of an activating energy flow-pure force. Palms up - form.

Palms down - force. Form and force together (one palm up and the other down) create stress for growth. We cannot have one without the other. Certain sephiroth on the Tree of Life are more receptive in their energy operations; others are more activating.

The chart which follows can be a guideline for hand positions when performing circle dances to activate the specific sephiroth.

Sephira	Force/ Form	Palm Position	Rotations
Kether	Both	Right down, left up	One
Chokmah	Force	Both down	Two
Binah	Form	Both up	Three
Chesed	Form	Both up	Four
Geburah	Force	Both down	Five
Tiphareth	Both	Right down, left up	Six
Netzach	Force	Both down	Seven
Hod	Form	Both up	Eight
Yesod	Both	Right down, left up	Nine
Malkuth	Both	Right down, left up	Ten

With the palms down, the energy radiates outward. With palms in a raised position, the energy is drawn within. When alternated, right palm down and the left up, there occurs a balance between form and force in the flow of energy activated by the hand movements. This balance occurs naturally with those sephiroth of the Middle Pillar.

If the sephira is one of *force,* then the dance should be performed in a deosil or clockwise direction. If the sephira is one of *form,* then it should be performed in a widdershins or counterclockwise direction. These clockwise and counterclockwise movements should bring to mind the workings of the machinery of the universe, which you as the dancer are setting in motion.

If the sephira is one of those of the Middle Pillar combining force and form, the direction can be determined by the specific purpose. If it is a group dance, the group can be divided into two sets of performers - a circle within a circle. One group would dance clockwise, and the second counterclockwise. This intensely amplifies the energy invocation.

There is often some question as to how many circular rotations to make to activate the energies of the sephira when circle dancing. This varies, but by using the chart above, the most simple way of determining and remembering it (while giving it appropriate significance) is by the numerological correspondence associated with the particular sephira. For example, for the sephira Hod the individual or group would dance the circle eight times.

After the dance itself, there should be time for the assimilation of the energy. The simplest technique is to step inside the magic circle that has been marked out by the dance. There the individuals assume a meditational pose, absorbing the energy and experiencing it being set in motion to manifest, according to its purpose within the physical life. Assuming one of the positions or *attitudes* as described below is an effective means of enhancing this. Remember that we are using the physical movements to stimulate specific responses. The more significance we give them, the more they can work for us.

When we complete the raising of the energy through dance, we then assimilate and focus it through the meditation. This then brings us to the point of releasing it to work for us within our physical life. Before leaving the meditational pose or physical attitude, give thanks to the universe, in advance, for its manifestation into your life. Step back to the edge of the magic circle, and dance an equal number of rotations in the opposite direction. This opens the circle, releasing it to begin its work for you. Bow to the bindu, and take three steps backward. Your ritual is completed.

Physical Attitudes

Prostrate

This is grounding of the energies activated by the dance. With outstretched arms, it becomes serpentine (as in the Serpent of Wisdom within the Tree of Life). The prostrate position can also be semi-prostrate, as in the yoga position of the cat's stretch, with arms outstretched and the knees tucked under. Womblike in appearance, the dancer gives birth to new energies through dance. It is a position of personal negation - an acceptance of divine authority. It is an excellent position to use when reaching for the objective at the bindu or center of the sephirotic circle.

Kneeling

This position, when done on both knees, represents the human ascent toward divinity while still attached to the Earth. When assumed on one knee, it indicates an increase in freedom - partial resurrection through the divine energies activated in your life by the dance. (Genuflection signifies our status in relation to those beings of the archangelic realm who work with us as guides.)

Standing

This position signifies us now able, through the energies invoked, to be upright and able to move. It signifies the emergence into a body of light, accomplished through the energies of the dance. It is also symbolic of being able to now tread the path upon higher levels. We can climb the Tree to even greater heights.

Sitting or Resting

This position is one of outer quiet with great inner activity-the activity of the levels of consciousness stimulated by the dance. It is representative of the changing of energy from one state to the next. It is a position of closure and receptivity, especially effective for those sephiroth whose energies are form.

With all of the sephiroth, any of these physical attitudes would work following the dance. The important factor is to find significance for all physical activity. Through the physical movements, gestures, and postures, we are learning to transcend the physical and link it with the spiritual.

Spinning the Tree into Existence

A powerful technique for using circular movements to awaken the Tree of Life within us is by creating the vortex. Energies that we are trying to access operate at a higher vibration than physical energies. With spinning, we speed up our own energy centers, our chakras, so that we can more easily and consciously access the energies.

Our chakras mediate all energy into and out of the physical body. Although they are not part of the physical body, they are intimately connected to it, linking our subtle energies to our physical consciousness. To access and ground higher vibrational energies, these centers need to function more fully and completely. One way of speeding up our own vortices or chakras is through whirling motions.

Whirling loosens the etheric webs so that the energy flowing into and out of the physical body and consciousness is stronger and more vital. It has a vitalizing effect. When combined with proper visualizations, it enhances meditative work with the Qabala. Whirling can be taken to extremes, beyond what is accomplished by some of the whirling dervishes. When extreme, the effects are detrimental. Chakras become over stimulated and imbalanced. This releases unbalanced psychic energy, which is often taken as a spiritual experience. It can loosen the etheric body from the physical so that it allows free access by other energies and entities without your control.

Whirling as is taught here is effective in speeding up the energy centers to elicit an easier access to levels of energy and consciousness that are not normally so accessible. Remember that dance is used in a controlled manner to access the energies of our spiritual consciousness. And more is not necessarily better. Just because you may feel the effects after a certain number of revolutions does not mean that increasing the revolutions will increase the effects. Some feel when they have used this technique for a while that the effect is lost. They do not seem to feel it as strongly as they did initially. This is usually a positive sign of growth. It indicates that your energy has grown, and your vibrational rate of the past has now increased and is maintaining a higher rate. This is not an indication to increase the revolutions to recapture those first feelings.

In essence, the individual has become acclimated to the higher vibrational rate, which is now the norm. Yes, we do want to continue to increase our energy, but this is now more likely to involve a change in techniques rather than an increase in the speed of the old techniques. We may still use the old techniques, if only for the mind set they create in preparing. They will always help align the physical so that the energies can be more fully experienced.

Creating the Vortex

1. Stand erect with arms outstretched. Focus your attention on the appropriate sephira. Know how many revolutions are necessary to activate the energy of the sephira (e.g., Netzach = eight).

2. Hold the palms in the appropriate position.

3. Visualize yourself in the middle of a sacred circle. You can even create your own by walking a small area around you. As you do so visualize it filled with the color of the sephira with which you will be working.

4. Visualize yourself as the magical image for the sephira. Feel the energy start to come alive. Know that while assuming this image with this exercise, you become the magician. You will create energy where there had been none.

5. Tone the Divine name for the sephira. This is a call to attention, and it activates all aspects of your being. Offer a prayer to the fulfillment of your purpose.

6. Visualize the archangel of the sphere standing guard over your activities and commence spinning the

appropriate revolutions.

7. Upon completion, assume one of the physical attitudes. Meditate upon the energies of the sephira that are now active within your life. To take this even further, visualize yourself entering into the Tree of Life and the appropriate inner temple, as you have already learned to do.

8. The spinning should *always* be done in a clockwise manner. (Imagine a clock, face up on the floor.) Doing it counterclockwise can activate the qliphoth, or negative energies of the Tree. The clockwise movement also speeds up the activities of our own chakras, so they can more easily mediate the higher energies. The natural direction for the rotation of the chakras is clockwise.

If dizziness becomes too strong, stop immediately. The number of revolutions is a guideline. With practice, the body will be able to handle the revolutions without the discomfort. With practice, you can learn to activate the energies of any sephira with only one revolution. You are learning to become the magician/alchemist. The important factor for now is doing something physical to correspond to the more ethereal energies you are accessing. As your own energy centers become acclimated to working with higher vibrations, the dizziness will no longer be a factor.

One can also spin the entire Tree into existence using this technique. You begin with one revolution - with proper visualizations - for Kether, move right to Chokmah and two revolutions, then on to Binah and three revolutions, etc. Assume each magickal images into yourself and visualize the colors. This will bring the entire Tree of Life energies into play within your physical. It is an excellent prelude to deeper work with the Tree, and it provides excellent practice in visualization and the assumption of magical images (seeing, feeling and becoming the magical image). It facilitates being able to do it at will.

Specific Dances for the Sephiroth

Malkuth

Malkuth is at the foot of the Tree of Life. The exercises and movements associated with it stimulate the energies of the chakras within the feet. Many times, these chakras are ignored or given little credit. It is in fact the chakras in the arches of the feet that ground us and tie us to the energy of the Earth and all of its forces. Implied within this is the recognition that the Earth and its energies are what we must learn to use and control to assist us with our evolutionary spiral. If we are to activate the energies of the Tree of Life and bring them into play within our lives, then these centers must be more fully activated. We are trying to become a living Tree of Life, with our head in the heavens and our feet upon the ground. If our feet are not upon the ground, we are not a Tree. Rather, we become a tumbleweed when we set these energies in motion. We are trying to integrate all of our energies, and that means we must also integrate the forces of Earth with the forces of heaven.

In the past, students of metaphysics have focused strongly upon the seven major chakras and their effects and aspects within the evolutionary process. The modern student of the mysteries needs to become aware that there are actually Twelve Major Centers of Light to be awakened and utilized if we are to release our highest capacities.

The number twelve has always had much symbolism attached to it. The twelve centers, or major chakras of the body, can be likened to the twelve lights surrounding the manger, the twelve signs of the zodiac, etc. In the ancient Greek mysteries, twelve was the holy number. And two of the twelve centers are found within the arches of the feet. They involved helping man to become initiated into the Earth's mysteries and all of its energies.

Since Malkuth is at the foot of the Tree, the movements start with activating our own "foot" energies.

Malkuth

A.

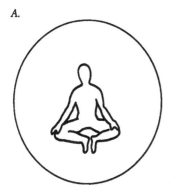

B.

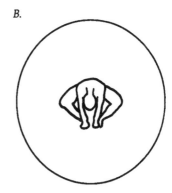

Activating the chakras in the feet so we can more fully work with Malkuth, at the foot of the Tree of Life.

C.

D.

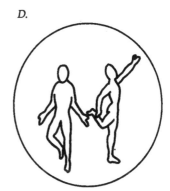

Acknowledging the energies of Malkuth in the Middle Pillar; and as the point of origin for dancing the Tree of Life.

E.

All that we need to grow and learn rests within the Kingdom of Earth (Malkuth).

Before coming to a rest, one can walk a square in a count of four, with each step at an angle or corner of the square, representing the energies in Malkuth that form the base of the Tree of Life.

Plants and trees grow from the bottom to the top. In Eastern philosophies, there is a belief that heaven is achieved through the feet. Learning to connect our energies with the energies of the Earth helps propel us to new growth.

Position A, sometimes referred to as "Butterfly," is very important. It brings the chakras of both feet together. By focusing our attention upon them in this position, we help activate them. As with all of the movements and postures, this creates electrical changes in the body, which in turn facilitate tapping the level of consciousness that is associated with it. In position B we bend forward, holding the feet, focusing our attention and energies even more strongly upon their activation. While doing this, think of yourself as a butterfly. A butterfly breaks free of the cocoon in order to fly free. Malkuth is where we learn this.

There is no set time to hold these positions; each individual must work that out. When you feel that your chakras in the feet are activated, then move on to the next. A good test is to stand up and feel the Earth with your feet. Bend them; flex them forward, back, side-to-side. Pretend you are walking while paying attention to your feet and their connection to the ground. How lightly can you touch the ground and still feel it? Can you hold your foot above the ground and feel the pull of gravity upon it? We are increasing awareness of the Earth and its energies to us.

In movement C, raise yourself up on your toes, hold and lower yourself into a squat position, remaining on your toes. Do not force the squat. Go only as far as is comfortable. Malkuth is part of the Middle Pillar. By rising up on the toes and then squatting down, we are raising our energies through Malkuth and bringing them down to Earth in a balanced manner. Movement should be slow and deliberate. Remember also that the more significance we can attach to the movements, the more they will do for us. Our higher self communicates to us through symbology, but communication must be two-way. We have to be able to respond. These movements and postures are symbols we send to the higher consciousness, because symbology is the only language it knows.

In movement D, we balance ourselves on each leg - feeling it, drawing it up into the dancer position. Through Malkuth, we enter the entire Tree, including all pillars and their sephiroth. With this movement we acknowledge that all energies end in Malkuth, and that we can explore all worlds through Malkuth. All that we need rests within the Earth/Malkuth, and thus we also rest (position E), balanced for our work.

Yesod

Yesod is the foundation. It is sometimes considered the doorway to the higher energies of the Tree of Life. It is associated on a physical level with the sacrum. Western humanity in general is very tightly hipped. We are not as flexible in the spine and hips as are other peoples throughout the world. We have tended to lock our energies in. On one level, these energies are sexual, but on their highest and truest level these energies are our basic life force. With these movements, we release the life force without it becoming sexual. At this level, we are dealing with primal life force not sexuality, so we want to have as much fun as possible with the movements. Life should be a celebration, and with these movements, we are celebrating the release of our life force for greater, more beneficial expression within our lives.

With movements A and B, we circle the hips in a crescent, or half-circle. This is, of course, symbolic of the Moon energies associated with the sephira of Yesod. Slowly we begin to widen the circle into a full Moon. The head should be loose and free; the spine and hips should be allowed to open up. Have fun with the movements. We are simply freeing up the energy locked in the sacrum, linking it with its corresponding level of consciousness.

Once the hips have opened up, place the dominant

hand upon the forehead and the other upon the sacrum itself, as in diagram C. We are taking the released energies of Yesod and the sacrum and using them to activate our higher abilities. We are taking life force energies, usually expressed through sexuality, and directing them for higher forms of creativity. Push the head back and push the hips forward slowly and deliberately. Take side-to-side steps while making this gesture. We are activating this energy to use it in any direction we desire. We control where, when, how much, etc. of this energy we express. All of this is inherent within the movements.

Finally, we end the dance with a Child's Pose. You are on your knees, with arms stretched out and head down. This is a humbling and reverential posture. It says that you recognize the divinity within all energy. You are acknowledging the divine source of the creative life force within you.

This reverential aspect is very important if we are to tap that level of consciousness known as Yesod in the most balanced manner. Yes, it does release energy, but unless it is treated with reverence, it manifests as an unbalanced expression, getting off track, slipping out of the Middle Pillar into an unbalanced manifestation of Netzach in the Pillar of Mercy. The vice or unbalanced expression of Netzach is lust. Again, we begin to see the interplay between one level of consciousness and the next, and we can begin to understand the need to treat each one individually until we are more aware of how they truly function.

The reverential aspect in this movement helps us to awaken greater independent expression of our own creative life force. We each are unique and have a unique way of experiencing the universe and its energies. Recognizing the divine spark inherent within our energies helps us to lay that new foundation and begin the process of becoming an independently creative life essence within the universe.

Yesod

A.

B.

In positions and movements A and B, we begin the process of freeing the blocked sexual/life force energy within our foundation (Yesod). We must remember that this is life force we are freeing and not treat it as sexual energy. We circle and half-circle (crescent Moon shapes) with the hips. Allow them to swing free and full. This technique will also deepen dreams and awaken psychic ability. Keep the head free and the whole spine loose, allowing the hips to gradually open up, wider and wider.

C.

D.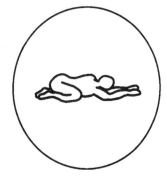

Place dominant hand on forehead and weaker on sacrum. As you push the head back, you also push the hips forward. Lift head and then bow, sanctifying the sexual/life force.

The Child's Pose balances the sacral center and gives reverence to its energy.

Hod

Hod is the sphere of Mercury. It is knowledge and communication. It is quick, abrupt movement and consciousness. Within it can be found the treasures of wisdom and knowledge and the applying of these in the material world. On a physical level, it is associated with the solar plexus chakra, which controls rational thinking. One of its primary symbols is that of the serpent (as in the caduceus), representing knowledge and wisdom on its lower level that will help us to reach the higher.

The movements associated with diagram A should be quick and abrupt. Mercury moves fast. While performing these movements, one should be able to feel the pull in the solar plexus area as the physical movements themselves tighten the stomach muscles in that area of the body. Initially, stand with the toes about forty-five degrees apart, heels touching. Then walk in small circles, taking steps of about forty-five-degree angles, which will look like Charlie Chaplin movements. This Chaplin fun-walk gives the appearance of jerky, abrupt movements - Mercury-like. It also strongly activates the energy of the solar plexus. Then switch the position of the heels and toes, with toes together and heels apart. You will look pigeon-toed. Again, walk in small circles. You will feel the solar plexus, which will enable you then to more fully access that level of consciousness most closely associated with it-Hod. Have fun with it.

In diagram B, we see a picture that is symbolic of the position of Hod upon the Tree of Life. It is at the base of the Pillar of Severity. The squat position on the toes symbolizes the energy of Hod at the base (squat) of its own pillar. Then, in a slow, very deliberate movement, imitate a serpent motion to bring yourself to a standing position, with heels firm and flat upon the ground. Do this several times. Learning raises us up and builds a firm foundation for even greater expressions of energy.

The last movement is the cobra posture of yoga. The serpent is the serpent of knowledge and wisdom that is

Hod

A.

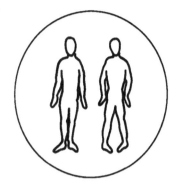

The Chaplin fun-walk and pigeon-toed movement are very stimulating to the solar plexus chakra, which helps link us to the level of our consciousness known as Hod.

B.

Hod is at the base of the Pillar of Severity. Knowledge lifts us up and plants us firmly in our paths, symbolized by these movements.

C.

The Cobra is the epitome of the Hod postures. We become the Serpent of knowledge, seeing where it is that we yet have to go, lifting our eyes and our lives to the higher.

available to us at that level of consciousness known as Hod. This posture helps open that level of our consciousness even more strongly. Lie flat on the ground, face down. See yourself as a snake lying there. Slowly lift your head to see more clearly, to rise to the higher. Place elbows under you, rising and lifting the head even higher. Finally, with head back, looking up as high as possible, stretch the arms up and hold the position of the cobra, poised. Remember, knowledge lets us see what we still have ahead of us and beyond us and shows us the way to achieve it.

Netzach

Netzach is the green sphere of Venus. It is the sphere of love and attraction, and the sphere of nature and emotions. It is the sphere of sexual energy that draws others to us with all the blessings that can come through other people. The movements associated with Netzach help us activate the level of our consciousness that helps us to attract love and quick rewards. This is not a thinking level of consciousness, but a feeling one.

Netzach is very important to dancing the Tree of Life. It is the center of art and creativity. Haniel, the archangel to whom we have access at this level of our consciousness, is sometimes considered the patroness of the arts. When we dance the Tree of Life through any of these movements, we are using an art form to work with the energies of the Tree. We are using the energies of Netzach to open up the entire Tree. The movements reflect the microcosm of the entire Tree.

We can do this with other levels as well. We also are learning to work with the Tree from an intellectual aspect, approaching it from the level of Hod. We are learning to be free in our approach to the energies within us, learning to express them and ground them in a balanced and yet creative manner. We are consciously (Hod) using specific movements and dance forms (Netzach) to access greater

Netzach

A.

Movements should be slow and expressive, as if coaxing new energy into your life. Arms and hands are invoking with love and joy. All movements and gestures should be inviting, as if pulling life to you. It is as if you are sending out magnetic energy, attracting life to you. You are drawing the fruits you need out of the Tree.

B.

This posture has you open, spread, ready to bring into you that which you need and want. From the upright position, sway side-to-side, moving your arms as if pulling energy into your life in the physical.

C.

The Triangle posture is very effective. Focus on the extended hand with your eyes up. We are invoking, coaxing energy and new growth to us. It also reflects that all of the energies we invite to us through Netzach from elsewhere on the Tree are to the right and above, or below and to the right (Malkuth—hand on the foot).

levels of energies. Using both balances us more fully, touches us more intimately, as the two meet in the middle. The Pillar of Mercy, with its base in Netzach, and the Pillar of Severity, with its base in Hod, meet through the conscious use of movement in the Middle Pillar, with its base in Malkuth (our physical life and consciousness).

Netzach is the sphere of Nature, and Nature is free-flowing, which is how the initial movements *(A)* should also be. Move slowly and freely, swinging the arms and hands as if coaxing an invisible person into your presence. This is often how Venus affects us astrologically; we are mimicking it. The eyes should also coax. In essence, through the dance, we are coaxing and inviting into our lives those things we treasure and love, be it people or things. We are activating those energies within our consciousness which can bring them to us! It means also that you are putting yourself into the flow of Nature, so that it can bring you that which you treasure and love, at the time most beneficial.

Humans are not always in synch with Nature and the rhythms of the universe. This free-flowing movement enables us to start realigning ourselves with the inflow and outflow of natural tides in the universe and in our lives. The eyes are also important. Tantra teaches different types of gazes, in conjunction with releasing specific energies. One of these is called the "conjuring" or "coaxing" gaze, in which the eyes are turned to the right and upward while holding the breath. This is significant for Netzach. In the Tree, Netzach is placed at the bottom of the left-hand Pillar. This means that all the rest of the energies that can be manifested through that level of our consciousness are positioned either to the right or above upon the Tree of Life. The eyes also have nerve structures that are unique to the body and similar to the brain. Particular eye movements stimulate specific brain responses. In this case, they align our energy patterns to the Netzach level of our consciousness.

For some, the posture of the second movement may be difficult. One sits in a position that is wide open, and which for many speaks of sexuality. In essence, though, it is a posture that symbolizes the openness of the person to receive the treasures they love. For most people, treasures usually take the form of a physical and tangible manifestation; thus the use of a blatant physical posture. But we must remember that these are simply bridges to help us manifest in our lives that which we need and desire.

Again, the side-to-side swaying is important, using the arms as if to pull into your life that which you love. Venus is the love goddess. No one can resist her charms. This movement is saying that nothing can resist you; you are drawing all the treasures of life into your own. All that is meant to be a part of your life and your world can be so if we invite it and not force it. Let nature bring it to you in the time, manner and means that are best for you. We are learning to trust Mother Nature as she operates fully within our lives.

The third position is the yoga posture known as the Triangle. Netzach is the seventh sephira. Seven is numerologically comprised of a three and a four. The four is the base, and the three is the Triangle, of greater power within the foundation of physical life. This position is more abstract and symbolic than the other two. And the more symbolic and abstract the symbol, the higher the level of energy we can access. Yes, we can activate much energy on a mundane level, but we also need to go beyond that. This posture opens the door to experiencing the energies of Netzach on an even higher level. Through Netzach we coax and invoke all that we love from everywhere in the universe. This is symbolized by the posture of the Triangle. Everything on the Tree of Life is, as mentioned, either above to the right or below and to the right of Netzach. This posture has the hand extended to the right (for everything we invite from that side of the Tree). It also has the eyes focused up to invite all that is above Netzach in the Tree. The posture also takes the energies it invites and grounds them into manifestation into the physical, as with the hand upon the foot.

This can be used specifically when linking and inviting energies from another particular sephira. For example, if new teachers and new learning are desired, alter the extended hand to point to the appropriate level of the Tree, in this case Hod, and visualize it being drawn to you, as in a ball of orange or whatever the appropriate color may be.

Netzach is that which we love and desire, and physical movement is a powerful way of drawing it to us. Shamans have used similar techniques in the past and present, such as in the inviting of rain. It must be remembered though that the universe is a cosmic reservoir of abundance, and this technique should never be used to interfere with the free will of another. Even that which we desire must be balanced, or it becomes a lust - be it for another person or for more material things.

Tiphareth

Tiphareth is at the heart of the Tree of Life. In the human body it is associated with the heart and the heart chakra. Tiphareth is the center of the Christ energy in the universe and within us. It is the little child, the sacrificed God and the King. From Tiphareth, one can reach out to all other levels within the Tree. It is the balancing center, the healing center for the physical and for the spiritual. When we bring its energies to play within our lives more actively, there results greater health and greater devotion to God.

Tiphareth is located in the middle of the Middle Pillar, which has much significance and power. It balances, as does our own heart chakra. The heart chakra has three chakras below and three above. It is by activating fully the heart chakra that we can begin to more fully open the upper chakras for even greater spirituality within our lives. It is here that we learn to sacrifice the lower for the higher, but only so that our own light may shine more strongly within the world. It is at this level of our consciousness that we stop looking for the Divine Light to shine down upon us and learn to bring to life our own light, so that the divine can shine out from us.

The movements and postures are designed to effectively stimulate the heart chakra and its corresponding level of consciousness. This in turn releases healing energies into our lives, first so we can see what needs to be healed, and second so we can heal it. They are energizing movements, and once they have been done a number of times, you will not quite feel balanced until you have done them again. This is because of the stimulating effect they have on the heart chakra. Sometimes we become acclimated to our imbalances, and thus may even deny we are in such a condition until we feel ourselves back in balance. Then we recognize the condition we had ignored.

The first exercise, "Activating the Inner Sun," is a good one to do periodically throughout the day. It keeps the heart chakra energy active. It can be done from any position and in any place - at the office or at home. With your dominant hand (we will use the right), rub the area of the heart in small circles. This stimulates the thymus gland, the heart rhythms and the entire heart chakra. It is soothing to the emotions and calms and balances the inner systems.

Next, take the right hand and draw the energy of the heart (inner Sun) to the head to activate the higher levels of consciousness. With the left hand placed over the heart, pause and contemplate the linking of the divine love with divine thought. Then draw the right hand back down and place it over the left upon the heart. This is a very calming gesture. A good confirmation of its actual effect is to place the hand over the heart to feel the heart beat before you do this exercise; then feel the heart beat at the end. You will notice a difference!

The next exercise is taken partially from oriental tai chi and adapted for these purposes. There are different breathing techniques utilized in tai chi. Two such techniques are the Sun and Moon breaths. With the Sun breath, you exhale slowly, extending the arms forward in front of the

Tiphareth

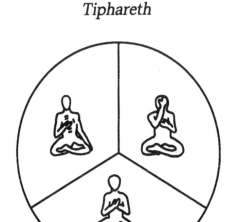

A. Activating the Inner Sun
—*Massage the area of the heart chakra with the right hand (circular motions).*
—*Place left hand over heart, and with the right hand bring the energy of the heart and inner sun to the head.*
—*Bring right hand down on top of the left over the heart area.*

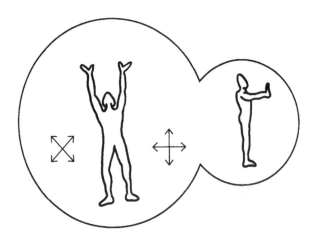

B. The Solar Breath
—*As you exhale, slowly push arms out in the six different directions. You are becoming a living Sun, radiating from the heart in all directions.*

chest, with the palms of the hands facing outward. We are pushing the energy of the inner Sun out into *our* auric fields. The Moon breath is an inhalation, drawing the arms and energy into you with the palms of the hands facing inward. Take a few moments, practicing both. You will feel the energy moving out and drawing in. It is very invigorating.

During this version of it, as depicted on the following page, we are trying to radiate our energy in six directions (Tiphareth being the sixth sephira): up, down, to both sides and at diagonals, and finally forward. (Or north, south, east, west, etc.) It is done with six basic movements, exhaling audibly with each. The arms raise up, pushing the energy up and out. Then they move down, pushing the energy down and out. Next, the right arm is extended out to the right and the left arm to the left. After each movement, bring the arms together, with the hands in prayer position at the heart. Inhale to gather the energy in the heart area before radiating it outward.

Next the arms are moved in a diagonal position, with one hand pushing energy diagonally down and the other diagonally up, moving in unison with each other. Then they are switched. The one that moved diagonally down now radiates the energy diagonally up, moving in unison with each other. Then they are switched. The one that moved diagonally down now radiates the energy diagonally up, etc. The hands move back to prayer position at the heart for the final and sixth movement. The arms extend with palms facing out, and the Sun within you bursts into radiant light around you. Visualize it, feel it and know it is real! You have become the Sun.

The yoga exercise on the following pages is known as the Sun Salutation. It is a series of movements that pays reverence and tribute to the Sun of the World and to the Sun within - macrocosm and microcosm. It consists of twelve basic movements - one solar year - but it must be done twice, for the right and left legs (diagrams D and I).

Stand facing the Sun or the east, from where the Sun rises. Circle your arms out and bring them into prayer position at the chest. You are acknowledging the sacredness outside of you and within you, which is what this whole series is for. Next (B) extend your arms and head up and back, looking toward the heavens and the stars (suns) that exist there and light up our night sky. Then slowly bend forward (C), bringing the hands down to the outside of the feet to touch the ground. Do not feel you have to keep your legs straight. Bend them and squat if necessary. You are bringing the Sun and light from the heavens to the Earth. It has filled your hands and you are passing it on to the Earth through them. In this case, the hands become the side pillars and the legs the middle pillar by which you were able to reach the Sun.

Now step back with the right leg (D). The head raises up, always looking toward the Sun. We are bringing the energy into motion with this, but only so that we can look at the Sun even more. As long as our face is towards the Sun, there will be no dark. Feel the Sun upon your face!

Step back with the other foot (E). You are now supported on your hands and feet. Keep the head up, toward the Sun. If you cannot support yourself this way, use your knees. This movement is to help us remember that we must attain the strength and support of the Higher Light within our lives and allow it to support us. At times, while in the physical, it may be the only strength and support we may have-but it is always enough.

Next, lower your knees and chest while raising the buttocks into the air (F). This position is very humbling. Through it we acknowledge that our own light, no matter how great we think it is, is humbled before the Light of Lights.

We now assume the cobra pose as we did in the sephira of Hod. In this posture (G), we are like a snake that has basked in the Sun and must now rise up to its own work. So we lift ourselves (H), pulling up from the involutionary, gravitational pull of the Earth to the evolutionary, spiritual force of the Sun. We become active

The Sun Salutation

A.

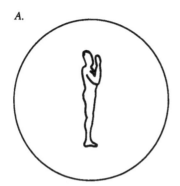

Circle arms into prayer position at the Christ center.

B.

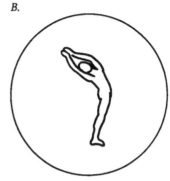

Acknowledge stars (suns) in heavens.

C.

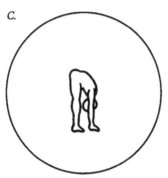

Bring the energy of the Sun to the Earth with the hands.

D.

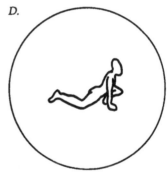

Leg steps back; head raises up—the face is always toward the Sun.

E.

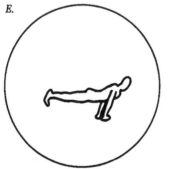

You must learn to let the Sun support you and give you strength.

F.

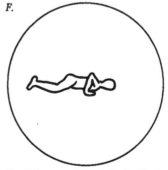

Our light—our Sun—is limited before the Light of Lights.

G.

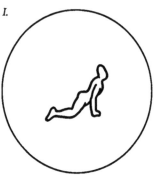

We begin to rise—like the cobra and the sun.

H.

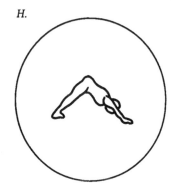

We lift ourselves from the Earth.

I.

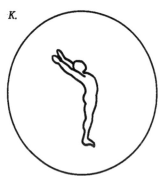

Leg steps forward between the pillars of arms, face to Sun.

J.

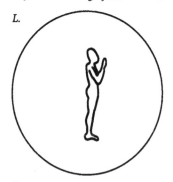

The Sun and the Earth are together again in you and through you.

K.

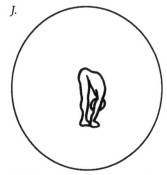

Acknowledge the Sun and stars throughout the universe.

L.

Your own Christ/Sun Center is alive within you!

again, so we step forward with the right leg (I), bringing it up between the pillars of the arms. We then unite within ourselves the forces of the Sun and the Earth, side by side, pillar by pillar. The Sun and the Earth forces are operating in you and through you.

You raise yourself up, lifting yourself and your energy to the heavens (K) to place your own Sun energy among the stars and suns of the sky, there to rest and shine (L). This completes half of the salutation. It must then be repeated, using the left leg to step back (D) and then to step forward as in step (I). Both sides must be done, or the Inner Sun will not be balanced.

Both sides align the Pillars, bringing them into balance and life in the Middle in Tiphareth. This activates strong electrical changes within - the body, enabling powerful contact with that level of our consciousness that we know as Tiphareth. For some, the moves may seem too much and too complicated, but we must remember that Tiphareth is at the heart of the Tree. It is the center to which we are striving so that we can then bridge to even higher levels still.

Geburah

Geburah is Mars energy. It is strength, courage and will. It is the warrior and the protector. It is the energy for the tearing down of the old. Through this level of our consciousness, we can stimulate energy to enact changes of any kind. It can be used to awaken critical judgment and for the attaining of information on the discord, however it may be manifesting, within our lives.

The movements are intended to stimulate greater feelings of strength and courage, and an awareness of innate power and energy. As with all energy, to be used properly, it must be disciplined and regimented. Its symbol is the chariot and the charioteer, who has control of the horses and their powerful strength. This is why the Horse Stance (diagram B opposite) is appropriate.

The first of the movements is "Marching to Mars" (A). Its function is to awaken the Mars energy and strength that is inherent within each of us. It is not a physical strength as much as a realization that we have an unlimited source of energy that we can utilize. Marching has always been a way for military groups to harness and discipline the energy and strength of a group. In this exercise, we are activating the energy of the Earth to more willfully direct it for higher functions. It begins by rising up on the toes and beginning a tapping cadence with the heels: up, down, up, down. We tap the heels in a cadence of five (Geburah being the fifth sephira), which stimulates changes in the physical body.

Five is the number for the pentagram, a symbol of tremendous energy. It activates energy in a specific pattern for work upon the physical. The tapping says that we are activating the energy for changes within our physical life.

As the heels tap, slowly raise the arms upward in a pumping motion in the same rhythm as the heel taps. It is as if they are being pumped upward by the energy released through the heels upon the Earth, like an air compressor. The hands are together so that the energy is controlled. Interlacing the fingers even further strengthens it. An interlaced set of fingers turns the hands into an instrument of war and strength.

When they reach the uppermost point above the head, separate the hands and swing them down and around, back to the chest, as if gathering in even more energy to concentrate. After the fifth sequence of these moves, begin marching in movements that are angular and not circular. Mars energy is sharp and direct. Pump the arms while marching, and either keep the hands in a fisted position or the fingers straight, extended and stiff.

Come to a rest in the Horse Stance (B). This is a common martial arts position. There is a slight bend in the knees, giving them flexibility. The fists are palm up and pulled back along the side of the ribs. You are balanced squarely upon both legs and should be able to move in any direction with ease. Lean forward, backward and side to

Geburah

A. Marching to Mars
—Raising up on the toes, begin tapping the heels against the Earth in a cadence of five.
—As heels tap, slowly raise arms upward in the same rhythm, as if being pumped up like an air compressor.
—On count of five the arms are circled down to the chest and begin pumping even stronger energy.
—After the fifth sequence, begin marching around the circle, pumping the arms and legs for even greater energy.

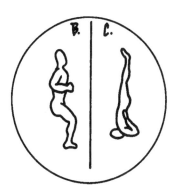

B. The Horse Stance
—Any typical martial arts stance is good. This is one of balance and strength with the energy pulled in, waiting to be set forth. Kick out as if kicking off what is no longer needed.

C. The Shoulder Stand
—This yoga posture is strengthening to the shoulders, associated with Geburah.

D. Reverse March
—A variation of (A). Heels begin cadence once more.
—Arms are circled out from the chest to an above-the-head position (gathering the Mars energy together).
—As the heels tap a cadence of five, the hands and arms are brought down to the chest.
—Do this five times.

209

side in this position to test your balance. Then begin kicking in all directions, to the sides, in front. Imagine you are kicking off the things you do not want in your life. Make the moves exaggerated but controlled. As you do this, see yourself ridding yourself of the things in your life you do not wish. Remember that Kamael, the Archangel of Geburah, defends the weak and helps us slay the dragons of our life. Visualizing Kamael behind you as you do this, giving energy to your kicks, is quite effective. Also, visualizing yourself as the magickal image for Geburah - the Mighty Warrior with his Chariot - gives it great power. Remember we are creating a mind set through physical actions to facilitate the accessing of that level of consciousness that corresponds to the energy of the physical. After the kicking, return to the Horse Stance again.

At this point, move into the "Reverse March" (D). Rise up on your toes and begin the cadence with the heels once more. Circle the arms upward from the Horse Stance to a clasped position above the head, pulling the energy down in rhythm with the tapping of the heels. As the heels tap the cadence of five, the hands and arms are brought down to the chest. They then circle out and up, to be brought down again to the cadence of five. After five repetitions of this, allow them to rest at the chest and proceed into the meditation you have chosen in relation to Geburah. You will have created the necessary changes in the energy patterns of the physical to attune it more to the metaphysical aspects of Geburah.

One can also use a shoulder stand or variations of the Plow of yoga as depicted in (C). This position is energizing and strengthening to the shoulders, which are in that area of the physical body associated with Geburah.

Find what works best for you. We are using the movements to bridge the mundane brain and consciousness to the more cosmic. Controlling how we do that is important. It is also an aspect of balanced Geburah energy.

Chesed

Chesed is the sphere of mercy and abundance. It is Jupiter. It is the seat of the Round Table. It is where we truly learn about our own quests for the Holy Grail and about all that we will need and have to achieve the quest. It is the level of our consciousness which lets us know that the universe is ruled with glory and magnificence. It lets us know that the majesty of the Divine operates in us all and thus all of us have access to everything which demonstrates that majesty.

Touching this level of our consciousness awakens a greater sense of obedience to the higher calling. It provides the energies to enable us to make the gains and opportunities beneficial to us. It awakens the realization of the abundance of the universe that exists for us all.

In order to tap that abundance, we must be willing to receive it. Unfortunately, we have developed the concept that being poor is the only way of being spiritual. We have developed a disproportioned martyr aspect that denies us abundance. If we have children, we want them to have all that they can. Yes, they may have to earn it, but they need to know that it is out there for them. We need to realize the same thing. We are the kings and queens of our own unique kingdoms, and that means that everything within it is already ours; and if it is ours, then we have the right to use it without feeling guilty.

Mercy is the quality of Chesed, and it begins at home. We have to have enough mercy toward ourselves to allow us to have all we need within our lives. Suffering is only good for the soul if it teaches us how not to suffer again. We must be willing to forgive and not punish ourselves by denying the abundance that is our right. Yes, it can become obsessive if unbalanced, but denying ourselves what is ours to begin with is imbalance as well.

Through Chesed we learn how to receive from the universe. We learn to share in the abundance of it so that we can do more to manifest the majesty and glory of God

Chesed

A.   B.

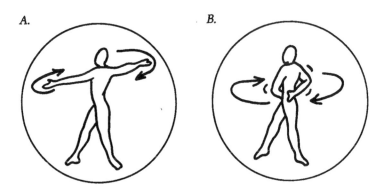

"Ropes of Abundance"

Figures A and B are movements that imitate the threads and ropes of life and how they are all tied together. The movements are circular, swinging the arms out and back around you, tying everything in the universe to you. You are not separate from anything; you are tied to the abundance of it all. The swinging frees us to receive that which we want, opening us to receive from the universe.

C.   D.

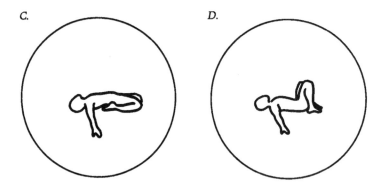

"Modified Fish"

This yoga position (C), as in its even more modified position (D), takes our legs away from us (tucking them under) so we have no choice but to depend upon and receive from the universe, from the heavens. We draw our true wealth from the heavens, not the Earth, and this position places us so that we have no choice but to receive, a task that is difficult for many people. Some people complain about the "uncomfortableness" of the position, and most of the time, it is because on some level they do not know how to receive. If (C) is too uncomfortable, position (D) can be used.

upon the Earth. Everything is available to us, but we must realize and be willing to accept it.

A king has much wealth in many forms, and a good king shares and distributes that wealth in many ways to those within his kingdom. The magickal image for this level of our consciousness is a crowned and mighty king, which is what we are trying to realize ourselves. We need to become that crowned and mighty king.

The exercises in this section deal with opening up that level of consciousness which allows us to share in the abundance of the kingdoms of Heaven and Earth. The first movements, (A and B opposite), are called the "Ropes of Abundance." Myths and legends from all over the world speak of threads that bind all things within the universe. They are connected to us and we to them. These movements are the setting in motion of the threads and ropes that tie us and link us to the abundance of the universe.

The movements are circular, swinging the arms in a wide, expansive manner, setting off ripples of energy around you to all comers of the universe. As we swing back, wrapping the arms around us, we are pulling on the ropes to bring to us the spiritual and physical abundance of the universe. We are linked to all things, and we are learning to claim our ties to it all. The swinging frees you and opens you to receive what you want and what you need.

In the next position (C), we tuck our legs back under us and lay back, open to receive from the universe. In essence, we are taking our limiting, earthly ideas and conceptions of abundance out of the way (tucking the legs back) so that we must open ourselves to receive from the heavens and their unlimited supply. We draw our true wealth from the heavens anyway, not the Earth, and this places us in a position in which we must receive. This is difficult for many to do, but this position almost forces an opening of that level of consciousness which will enable us to receive from the abundant universe.

Some people complain about the uncomfortableness

of position (C), and this is significant. Probably on some level the individual is made uncomfortable by receiving. Maybe they are the type of individual who does nothing but give to others, and won't take charity from outside. Maybe they refuse compliments. Maybe they only accept the big things and give no importance to the need to accept the small gifts, be they a compliment or an act of kindness. By doing this exercise in conjunction with the Ropes of Abundance, you **will** receive from the universe within the week. These gifts may be small compliments, little gifts, opportunities, etc., but it is important to accept them. Receive them thankfully. If we refuse to receive the small things, the universe certainly won't waste its energy on the larger. Let the universe know that you wish to share in its abundance. Accept everything it gives to you.

For those who find position (C) impossible or too uncomfortable, position (D) can be used until you become flexible enough to share even more in the universe.

All of these help us to open that level of consciousness that enables us to receive, so that we can expand our devotion and work. Gifts and opportunities come in many shapes and forms, and we must become as cognizant of them as possible, every day. Then we can know the magnificence of Chesed.

Binah

Binah is the archetypal mother. It is the womb from which physical life takes form. It is understanding which brings light into the dark. Its energies are not easy to access on their highest level, as it is part of the Supernal Triangle of the Tree of Life. Because of this, the movements and postures are less intricate and yet more abstract. They are simpler, and yet their significance is more complex. More can be read into the simple movements of Binah, Chokmah and Kether than into any of the other levels on the Tree of Life. We are beginning to work more closely with the pure essence of energy, which is not as easily definable as in the

Binah

With left hand on the womb and the right upon the heart (two female centers), slowly circle the head clockwise three times. This is followed by a slow circling of the trunk three times. Then the body leans forward, with a small soft gesture, signifying a coming forth from the womb. With the male, the hand positions are reversed as are the directions for the rotations of head and trunk.

"Old Tibetan Meditation Pose"
The individual takes a squatting position with the elbows resting upon the knees. The thumbs of the individual are placed in the inner corners of the eye, and the fingers of the hands are placed together in prayer position, forming a triangle over the third-eye area of the forehead. This position is then held. The length of time depends upon the individual.

lower levels of consciousness. This does not make them any more divine or powerful, but rather more difficult at times to relate to and work with.

Binah is Understanding on all levels and the silence that is necessary if we are to understand in the fullest manner possible. In the first two postures, we acknowledge the female energy in the universe. By placing our hand upon the womb and the heart, we are acknowledging that most of us will only be able to understand the working of the female energies in our lives upon the lower levels: through the creative process of giving birth through the womb and through the giving of love from our hearts (Binah being reflected down through the Tree of Life).

The circular rotations of the head release the energy of Binah, which is associated with the chakras of the head (particularly the third eye, which it shares with Chokmah). This released energy is then free to come to life more within our physical awareness, through the heart and the womb. The rotations of the trunk loosen the heart and the womb so they can more freely and fully express this archetypal energy. This series of movements is concluded by leaning forward. This is the giving birth of the energies throughout the Tree for greater expression - the coming out of the womb. We have circulated the energies, and now they must be given expression. The rotations number three, both for the head and the trunk. The forward movement is done only once. (Again this is just a guideline.) Three is the number of creativity and birth; and three is the number for Binah.

The positions of the hands will vary from individual to individual, particularly from females to males. Binah is a female sephira, a level of consciousness that works most fully with the feminine energies. A female performing these movements will do the circles in a clockwise direction, which moves energy out. This is significant, because the female already has the feminine energy awakened within her; it needs only to be set free. For the male, the movements will be in a counterclockwise position, and the hand placements will be reversed as well. The male is outside of the female energy of Binah; it is not as natural to him. Circling in a counterclockwise direction draws the female energy into him, activating it more strongly. Allow the movements and hand placements to be natural and comfortable. If it feels better to rotate clockwise, do so. If it feels better to keep the right hand upon the heart and the left upon the womb, then do so as well. Remember that we are trying to work and activate the expression of our energies in our own unique manner. These movements are to assist in linking with the corresponding level of our consciousness for its greatest expression within you.

The last posture is sometimes called the Old Tibetan Meditation Pose. In this posture, the individual squats first. Squatting was the proper position of giving birth in many ancient and even many contemporary rural societies. In a squatting position, the force of gravity facilitated the birthing process. In this meditation position, we are trying to give birth to clearer understanding.

The elbows rest upon the knees (Binah rests on top of the Pillar of Severity), and the thumbs of the individuals are placed in the inner corners of the eyes. Technically, this is the medial end of the eyebrow. This is a very powerful acupuncture and acupressure point on the urinary bladder meridian. It is a point used to stimulate the eyes for the relief of headaches and glaucoma and even for facial paralysis. It is stimulating to the brow chakra, the third eye.

The fingers of the hands are brought together in prayer fashion over the forehead, forming a triangle over the third eye area. The triangle is associated with the womb (the yoni in Eastern philosophies). It is a symbol for Binah. The triangle intensifies the energy of that which it surrounds (as in pyramid energy, etc.). The thumbs activate the third eye, and the fingers in a triangle over the area intensify it. Meditating in this position gives cleared insight and understanding (Binah). When one comes out of this pose, everything is physically clearer. It seems brighter, more distinct and sharper! We have energized our sight - physically and spiritually. We can now more easily tap our consciousness for higher understanding of other aspects of our life and begin to see how to give birth to even brighter light within it.

Chokmah

Chokmah is the archetypal father. It is the initiator. It is that level of our consciousness which sets things in motion. When linked with Binah, the archetypal female, new birth and life results. Chokmah is pure force pouring forth to manifest in myriad ways as it makes its way into our physical life. It is energy before energy takes a form of expression.

In movement A, stand with your eyes closed, your head hanging down. Brush your hands over your head, waking up the energy to set it in motion. Brush the hands slowly over the top of the head and the eyes. The hair hangs down. (As the energy of Chokmah asserts itself, it overflows to form Binah.) The eyes open slowly; again the energy is awakened and set in motion for greater manifestation.

Chokmah sets the wheels of life and the stars in motion within our lives. It opens a realization of our hidden abilities and energies, so that we can learn to start motion within our lives. The eyes slowly open, giving us this realization. We begin to see how the heavens, the universe and our own energies (the universe in miniature) operate on all levels.

Next we assume the position of the "half wheel." Sometimes it is called a back bend or a variation of the back bend. In it we are becoming the wheel of life. We are setting our energies and abilities into motion, getting things rolling. This posture links us with the angelic realms associated with this level of our consciousness. These are the *Auphanim*, or the "whirling forces."

Our faces and eyes are lifted up to Kether and

beyond. This is to remind us of the spiritual experience associated with tapping this level of our consciousness - a vision of god face to face. We look up to know how to best set our energy in motion.

Chokmah

Using the hands to sweep gently across the eyes as if to clear the sight is very effective. Cloudy gray is the color for Chokmah—the light hidden within the clouds. This motion moves the clouds away so the energy and light can manifest.

We awaken our energies by brushing our hands over our head. Our hair hangs down, the energies overflowing down to the rest of the tree. Our eyes open and lift upward, a growing realization of our hidden energies being brought to life and set in motion for greater manifestation.

"Half Wheel"

Chokmah sets the wheels of our energies in motion. We are becoming the wheel of life to initiate new energies into our life and to understand the workings of the wheels of the universe as they play upon us and through us. Our eyes look ever upward for the vision of God face to face, so we can know best how to use our energies with the highest wisdom (Chokmah).

Kether

Kether is the top of the Tree. It was the first to manifest out of the Nothingness and is the last that we touch before we enter into that Nothingness (that which we cannot know at all while in the physical). It is here that life and death meet. It is here that they become truly one and the same thing, and where we draw all sustenance for everything within our life. It is here that we can experience the unlimited reservoir of the divine operating in the universe.

Kether is not the end of our journey. It simply represents the end of a stage before the next level is undertaken. The Kether of one level of experience becomes the Malkuth of the next. One Tree of Life always leads upward into another - a Tree within a Tree within a Tree. In essence this is the climbing of Jacob's Ladder. Each rung leads to the next higher rung. Kether on one level of experience becomes the first step to an entirely new level of consciousness and the manifestation of our energies within it. The lower always bridges to the higher.

In position A, we are at the top of the Tree. We are reaching up and out from Kether into that which we cannot truly and fully know of while in the physical. Hold this position, even when tired. At this level, we are training ourselves to draw our focus away from the physical to the spiritual. Do not scratch; do not acknowledge any itches. We are transcending the physical, looking where there is no ache, no pain, no itching, and no scratching.

Slowly draw the arms downward, pulling the energy of the divine down into the physical to awaken new life and new strength to stimulate new energies of change and transition, and to be able to leave the past and go on to the future.

This means you must be able to put to rest that which is no longer beneficial. For this, assume the corpse pose (B). We die to one level of being only so we can be born to anew. In this pose, the energy we pulled down in essence

Kether

You are standing upon Jacob's Ladder, *A.*
the top of the Tree, looking out into the
nothingness, the source of all your essence.
Hold the position, even when tired. We
are trying to stretch our awareness from
the physical to the spiritual. You are
attempting to transcend the physical.

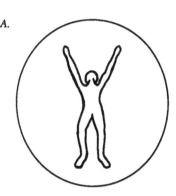

Slowly the arms lower, and the body *B.*
lowers itself into a corpse pose. We die to
one life that we may have a new. We are
attempting to become a part of the nothingness beyond Kether—beyond the
physical.

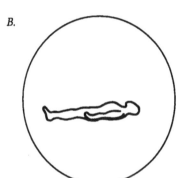

C. 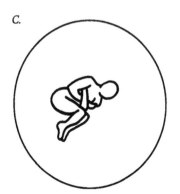 *D.*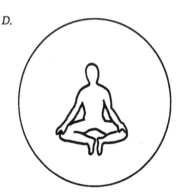

Out of the nothingness, we are born again,
coming back into life.

The Kether of one Tree becomes the
Malkuth of the next, and we start the
next spiral up!

raised us to become a part of the nothingness. Nothing is the space we wish to enter here. Visualize yourself free, floating in nothingness-no aches or pains. You are shedding the old before the new is once more taken upon yourself.

From the corpse pose, roll to your side to assume a fetal position. Out of death comes new life. We die to Kether to be born again to Malkuth. We come back into manifestation fresh, stronger, and ready to be born and to grow to yet greater heights.

From the fetal position, sit up (D) with the arches of the feet together, activating our new essence and stronger energy in Malkuth. The Kether of one Tree of Life becomes the Malkuth for the next higher. We are never lower than we have been before and we always go higher each time thereafter. Evolution is an ever-upward spiral. Acknowledge the feet and the energies of the feet chakras, for Kether has released new creativity for new steps in your journey of life.

Quick Guide to
Dancing the Sephiroth

1. Choose the sephira which contains energies you wish to awaken within you.

2. Decide on the particular effects within your life you wish this energy to bring about.

3. Set the atmosphere with candles, fragrances, etc. Take three steps to the center, where you have mentally placed your desire. Bow.

4. Begin the circle dance rotations (two steps forward and one step back). The number of rotations is determined by the number of *the* sephira. As you dance the magic circle, Tone the Divine name for that Sephira and begin to see the appropriate color build within the circle.

5. Complete the rotations, step into the circle and perform the balancing movements for the Tree of Life, given in the last chapter.

6. Then perform the dance movements for that sephira. As you do, imagine and feel yourself becoming the magical image of that sephira. *Be the image, dancing the movements!*

7. Visualize the temple around you and then reflect or meditate upon the objective, as if it is already working for you. Visualize and know that it is real. Hold the meditation until the realization of its fulfillment permeates your being.

8. Offer a prayer of thanksgiving for its manifestation in advance.

9. Move back to the circle's edge and dance an equal number of rotations in the opposite direction rotation to release the energy to work for you. As you do tone the Divine name and visualize the temple dissipating. As you do these last rotations, see and feel the energy pouring coming forth from the inner temple to your outer life to be fulfilled for you.

10. Perform the balancing movements. Bow to the center again and take three steps backward.

Chapter Ten

Dancing the Paths

Various movements and dances free our potentials and open us to messages and teachings, not as accessible before. We are trying to allow the Tree of Life to become a teacher to us and to communicate with us. Our higher levels of consciousness communicate to us through symbols, and if we wish to strengthen the connection and make it a two-way communication (to where we can call upon it at any time), then we need to learn to use symbols as well – including symbolic movements. If we are truly serious about clearing the bridges between the various levels of consciousness so that we have greater access to our innate potentials, then dancing the paths is critical to our Qabalistic work.

There are two very effective ways of doing this – each a little more intricate and a little more powerful than the other. I always recommend that we start simply. If you wish to get more creative and intricate, you can do so later, once you are more familiar with the process and the effects that it will elicit in your daily life.

The two easiest and yet most effective ways of dancing the paths are: The Walk to Knowhere and Dancing to the Stars. They each employ the same basic techniques as described on the following pages. But the process is simple. We start by awakening the first temple. Then we step through a door onto path we have chosen, that leads out from that sephira. We walk the path (using one of the two methods that you will learn here). Then we step through a door into the second temple and awaken it. And the more intricate we make the dance. the stronger we activate and release its energies, potentials and opportunities into our life. It may seem simple, but empowerment is not always complicated and does not need to be.

The Walk to Knowhere

The Tibetan Walk to Knowhere is a series of steps whose purpose is to induce an altered state of consciousness. It involves repetition of a set rhythm of steps: four steps forward and four steps backward. Forward, back. Inner, outer. This is actually one of the easiest and deceptively effective ways of dancing the paths.

The steps should be taken with full attention in a sure, slow and deliberate manner. With each step, place the heel down first and then the toes. This serves as an unconscious reminder to maintain a sure footing in your journey in life and upon the path you are now treading. The number of forward and backward movements varies. One method is to use the number of steps based upon the number of the path you are working. The path from Malkuth to Yesod - path 32 - then would take thirty-two forward and backward steps. To some this may seem a lot, but we must keep in mind that it initially takes more work to induce the altered state necessary to access the energies, especially at the bottom of the Tree. I have found though that when you are just beginning, stay with the basic four steps forward and four steps back.

Visualizing yourself as the magical image of the beginning sephira is also important. As you walk this path, visualize the path itself in the appropriate color. Find your own rhythm for the steps. As you step about halfway through the series, visualize yourself merging and becoming the magical image of the second sephira of the path. Now you are a combination of both magickal images, with the inherent power of both! This is tremendously powerful and energizing. It releases the energies of the path more intensely into the physical. It also helps you to develop concentration and creative imagination that can be used even more greatly for your benefit in the future.

The Walk to Knowhere Guide

1. Choose the path you will be working and review the energies associated with it.

2. Set the atmosphere-candles, fragrances, music, etc.

3. Perform the balancing postures to activate the Tree in the physical.

4. Perform the dance movements for the first sephira of the path, assuming the magickal image, using the Divine name to activate the temple.

5. Imagine stepping through a door at the back of the temple onto a path of the appropriate color. In the distance, you see what appears to be the second sephira or temple. (Imagine its color.)

6. Perform the Walk to Knowhere. As you do, imagine yourself walking along the path. You may even wish to imagine one of the archangels walking beside you on this journey to the second sephira.

7. Along the way, imagine encountering the gifts of the path and take them with you to the second temple. And bring

the Walk to Knowhere to a stop.

8. Imagine that you are standing before the second temple and the archangel of it appears at its doorway and greets you. Visualize yourself stepping in and perform the dance movements for the second sephira of the path, using the Divine name to activate the temple.

9. Imagine yourself becoming the magical image of this temple as well.

10. Assume one of the physical attitudes (discussed earlier in this part), and begin the meditational part of the pathworking – play the entire journey again in your mind.

11. Close the temples and the path by toning the Divine name of the first sephira, followed by the Divine Name of the second. Repeat three times, allowing the temple to fade from the vision.

12. Conclude with the balancing postures to ground and balance the energies stimulated into play by this pathworking. Know that you have activated the two temples and bridged them, bringing their energies out into your life.

Music for the Tree

<u>Sephira</u>	<u>Corresponding Music/Composers</u>
Malkuth	Anything of the home and hearth; Brahms' *Lullaby*; Dvorak; Puccini.
Yesod	Handel's *Water Music*; A Chopin *Nocturne* (anything that evokes deep feelings).
Hod	Woodwinds and horns; Mozart; Gershwin (rhythmic variety); Bach; Mozart's *Magic Flute*.
Netzach	Beethoven's *Pastoral Symphony*; Zamfir; Schumann; Mendelssohn.
Tiphareth	Handel's *Messiah*; Haydn's *Creation*; Pachelbel's *Canon in* D; Berlioz; sacred hymns.
Geburah	Marches of any kind; strong rhythms; Wagner's *Ride of the Valkyries*; Verdi's *Grand March*; *Pomp and Circumstance*.
Chesed	Franck's *Panis Angelicus*; Beethoven's *Fifth Symphony*; Tchaikovsky.
Binah	Bach-Gounod, *Ave Maria*; Schubert's *Ave Maria*; Brahms' *Lullaby*; Debussy's *Clair* de *Lune*.
Chokmah	Haydn's *Trumpet Concerto*; Rachmaninoff; Haydn's *Creation*; Vivaldi.
Kether	*Wagner's Pilgrim's Chorus*; *Theme from 2001: A Space Odyssey*; Pachelbel's *Canon in* D.

Playing these or other pieces of music that you choose in relation to the sephiroth adds even greater depth and power to the dance.

Dancing to the Stars

In more ancient times, the people and students of the spiritual sciences were very cognizant of the play of the heavenly energies upon the Earth and upon humanity. The imprints of the stars were a part of their life and their mind. If we are to truly awaken our highest consciousness and employ it fully within our world, we also need to become more cognizant of this. We need to re-imprint upon our physical brain the energies of the stars. The work with the Qabala and the dance movements can facilitate this for us.

A second very powerful and effective technique for dancing the paths is a process I call, "Dancing to the Stars". We can use physical movement associated with the Qabala to imprint upon our brain the movement and operations of the stars and planets. This will enable us to become more aware of their subtle and often ignored influences.

In the Qabala, we use symbols and gestures to awaken levels of our consciousness and link them together for greater use. There are constellations and planetary energies used as correspondences which enable us to decipher and understand the energies of our consciousness. These star and planet patterns are associated with both the sephiroth and the paths linked to them. We can use the constellation patterns to more fully bridge the levels of our consciousness by activating deeper levels of our subconscious, which are still capable of responding to those stellar influences.

On the following pages are the constellations and glyphs associated with the paths on the Tree of Life. These constellations and astrological glyphs serve as doorways to explore levels of our consciousness that otherwise could not be as easily explored. If we apply physical movements that mimic those symbols and constellation patterns, we bring to life more intensely the energies associated with them. We also bring out of our subconscious archives that ephemeral memory and attunement to the stars.

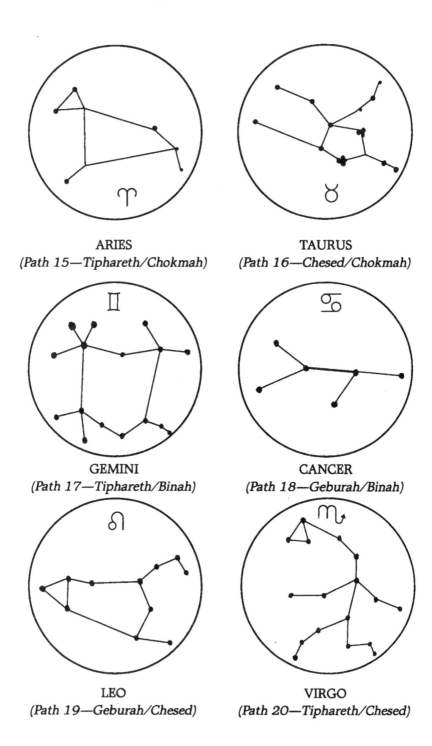

ARIES
(Path 15—Tiphareth/Chokmah)

TAURUS
(Path 16—Chesed/Chokmah)

GEMINI
(Path 17—Tiphareth/Binah)

CANCER
(Path 18—Geburah/Binah)

LEO
(Path 19—Geburah/Chesed)

VIRGO
(Path 20—Tiphareth/Chesed)

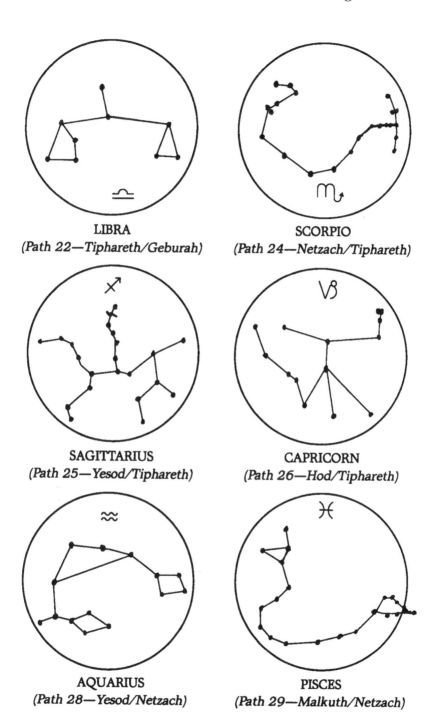

LIBRA
(Path 22—Tiphareth/Geburah)

SCORPIO
(Path 24—Netzach/Tiphareth)

SAGITTARIUS
(Path 25—Yesod/Tiphareth)

CAPRICORN
(Path 26—Hod/Tiphareth)

AQUARIUS
(Path 28—Yesod/Netzach)

PISCES
(Path 29—Malkuth/Netzach)

Physically stepping off the constellations associated with the various paths of the Qabala, and stepping off physically the astrological glyphs, heightens the consciousness associated with the pathworking. It enables you to become more physically sensitive to celestial movements and position within your life. It heightens our awareness of how astrological configurations influence and affect us on levels often not recognized. It awakens us to their gravitational influences on physical, emotional, mental and spiritual levels.

By physically dancing the constellations, we place ourselves in alignment with their rhythms, enabling them to work more fully for us and align our personal energies with the universal flow. The movements reflect the energies that will be released through the pathworking; thus they give the pathworking greater power.

Focusing upon the pathworking and dance at the appropriate time of the year for the astrological sign will elicit even greater benefits to the individual. If only working the twelve paths associated with the astrological signs, an individual can dance to the heavens in the course of one year! This opens a broad avenue for aligning the physical with the celestial. Ultimately, one could learn to dance the entire astrological chart, enhancing those aspects that are more beneficial. This can be used to smooth over those aspects of the astrological chart which are more difficult to handle in the physical. The movements of stars are so intimately connected to life in the physical that great strides could be made on any level by anyone wishing to choreograph it.

The process is the same as in the Walk to Knowhere. Instead of doing the repetitive steps though, you simply walk the outline of the astrological glyph associated with that path. This may be the glyph or you can even use the constellation pattern. (And yes, occasionally, you do have to backtrack when following the constellation pattern – but that can have significance as well.)

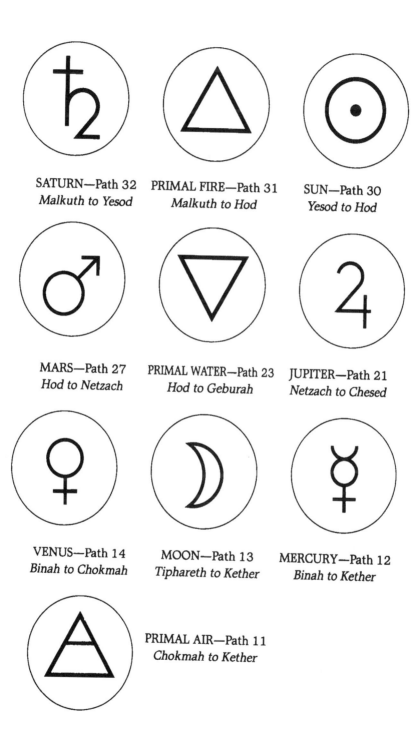

SATURN—Path 32
Malkuth to Yesod

PRIMAL FIRE—Path 31
Malkuth to Hod

SUN—Path 30
Yesod to Hod

MARS—Path 27
Hod to Netzach

PRIMAL WATER—Path 23
Hod to Geburah

JUPITER—Path 21
Netzach to Chesed

VENUS—Path 14
Binah to Chokmah

MOON—Path 13
Tiphareth to Kether

MERCURY—Path 12
Binah to Kether

PRIMAL AIR—Path 11
Chokmah to Kether

Imagine the path as having the outline of the constellation. Imagine its outline on the floor in the area where you are performing the pathworking. (Use the guidelines and charts on the following three pages.)

You may simply walk them, dance them, or spin around the area in the astronomical or astrological configuration. As you do so, see its outline being formed upon the floor in the appropriate color for the path. For example, if you are performing a pathworking for the 24th Path (Netzach to Tiphareth), you would dance an outline of the constellation of Scorpio. Envision it upon the floor in the color of green-blue.

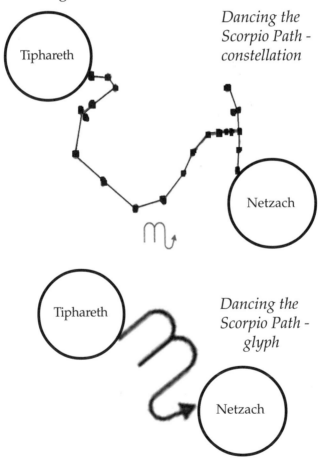

Dancing the Scorpio Path - constellation

Dancing the Scorpio Path - glyph

Advanced Pathworking to the Stars

As discussed earlier, the path associated with your astrological sign holds much significance in your life lessons, as does the path of the planet that rules your astrological sign. The element of your sign (Air, Fire, Water or Earth) can give even further revelations.

One method of working with dance and the Tree is to focus on these three aspects and paths each month. For example, work the paths for Cancer, the Moon and Water during June and July, when the sign of Cancer is most active in the year. In a year's period, you have basically danced the celestial energies into greater activity. This helps you learn to use and control them according to more universal rhythms so that they work more effectively for you.

A variation of this can be employed to activate energies around your birthday. Three aspects of the astrological chart which are very powerful are our Sun sign, the rising sign or Ascendant, and the Moon sign. A very powerful method of reactivating those forces in our life for the coming year is to path work their associated paths for one week ahead of your birthday. The birthday is a powerful time in a person's life. The inherent potentialities of our physical life are more active. Using the pathworkings will bring those energies into even greater manifestation

1. Seven days prior to your birthday, perform the pathworking for your Sun sign. Two days later, perform the pathworking for your rising sign, and two days later, that for your Moon sign.

2. The next day is your birthday, and it is a time to meditate on that which you want to manifest in the coming year.

3. You can also do this with the Sun sign, the ruling planet and the element as previously described. Either way, we are using three aspects - three paths. Three is the creative number. It is the birth-giving vibration in the universe,

which is more than significant for what we are doing.

It is also a good idea to occasionally dance the movements for the constellation associated with your astrological sign. This keeps you in touch with your basic energy pattern; it is usually when we lose this link when imbalance manifests. This keeps us grounded and in a position to more easily evolve into new energies.

Outdoor Pathworking

Pathworking lends itself very well to outdoors. If you can find an area (pasture, field, woods, etc.) with two trees a good distance apart, it is more effective. It will accelerate the play of that path's energies into your life. In a wooded area, the trees become antennae to link the play of celestial energies more acutely to the physical. They stimulate our natural intuitive aspects and the natural world helps us experience altered states in a more balanced fashion. You can walk the astrological path between the trees or even perform a more theatrical working.

1. Choose the path you wish to perform outdoors (any can be used). Review the energies associated with it.

2. Having arrived at your outdoor location, perform the balancing postures to activate your inner Tree of Life.

3. At the first tree - representing the first sephira of your pathworking – call it into being with the Divine name. Perform the movements for that sephira. When the temple comes alive, assume the magickal image and perform the dance for the beginning sephira of the path around the base of that tree.

4. Assume the meditational posture, and visualize yourself in the inner Temple. Allow yourself to be greeted by the archangel. Visualize a doorway from it leading out to the second sephira of the path in its appropriate colors

5. Open your eyes and rise. Now you are going to walk in that field or woods. You are physically walking the path. Walk in the pattern of the appropriate constellation or astrological glyph. Feel yourself in the presence of the archangels. Carry on mental conversations upon how you wish the energies of this path to play m your life. Be open.

6. Halfway through your "stroll to the stars," encounter the archangel of the second sephira. Know that you are now in the company of both.

7. Continue the walk until you have reached the end of the outline for the constellation or glyph - at the second tree.

8. At this tree - representing the second sephira of your pathworking – call it into being with the Divine name. Perform the movements for that sephira Assume a meditative pose, and meditate upon entering into the second sephira of the path, thereby completing the pathworking. Feel yourself becoming its magickal image.

9. Close the temples and the path by toning the Divine name of the first sephira, followed by the Divine Name of the second. Repeat three times, allowing the temple to fade from the vision.

10. Conclude with the balancing postures to ground and balance the energies stimulated into play by this pathworking. Know that you have activated the two temples and bridged them, bringing their energies out into your life.

Part V -

Secret
of the
Hidden Paths

Chapter Eleven

Secret of the Hidden Paths

When we begin to bridge the various levels of our consciousness through pathworking, we are inviting a whole series of initiations. These will manifest through the normal experiences within the day to day life. This is why most of the ancient masters taught their students and disciples to be ever watchful. Our greatest growth does not always come with easily recognized spiritual beeps and buzzers, alerting us to pay attention. Our growth occurs through daily life circumstances. When we work with the Qabala, we are developing the ability to observe the subtle interplay between our spiritual activities and our mundane life circumstances.

Pathworking shows us both common and uncommon relationships in our lives. In order though to recognize them for what they are and to assist our expanded awareness through them, watchfulness is absolutely necessary. The symbols on the paths and throughout every aspect of the Tree of Life reflect specific energies of the universe. When we learn to consciously use them in a specified manner, those abstract energies come into very tangible expression within our lives. Remember the axiom: *"All energy follows thought!"*

Pathworking triggers an awareness of synchronicity within our lives. Synchronicity, as described by Carl Jung, is when events coincide relatively within the same period and cluster around a central dynamic or value which gives meaning to the whole. In other words, things will happen in the time, manner and means that is best for us if we allow them to. We do what we can and must and then allow the events to play themselves out appropriately.

With pathworking, as in life, experiences with the good and those that are testing will occur and should be expected. Greater power will be given to see how we handle it. Temptation in many forms will arise. Tests of character and stress will be encountered, and our values will be challenged both inwardly and outwardly within our life. By working the paths on the Tree of Life, we are inviting the tests so that we can attain the rewards.

And rewards of both the spiritual and mundane should be expected. Both will manifest clearly and strongly. Greater power will be given in all situations of life. Our vision and perceptions will increase tremendously. We will find that which we thought beyond our control is no further from us than we allow it to be. We will see the reality of our dreams, and we will know the joy of setting them in motion and re-creating our life along any lines we desire. We discover that we are never given a hope, wish or dream without also being given opportunities to make them a reality. That is the journey of life.

Preliminary Cautions about the Hidden Paths

Pathworking is a means of inviting initiation into our life. It is a way of inviting tests and opening to the rewards of those tests. But there are always free variables – aspects of pathworking that can not be controlled. This is particularly true when working with the hidden paths. The built in protections and guidance on these paths are not as discernible sometimes as in the traditional paths.

Before delving into these 16 hidden paths, it is *highly recommended* that you be thoroughly familiar with all of the Sephiroth and have performed all of the traditional 22 paths on the Tree of Life. Remember that the idea is to control what you set in motion within your life. Pathworking will help create opportunities, but you must still face them and take advantage of them.

If you have issues surrounding a gift you hope to attain through a pathworking, those issues will likely be brought to the forefront to give you an opportunity to deal with them more successfully.

Spiritual energies activated through pathworking will intensify the daily, mundane circumstances of life – often forcing a reconciliation or resolution of daily troubles and problems. You will likely have to face your fears, doubts, limitations and perspectives that create barriers to manifesting the gifts that are inherent within us. Qabalistic pathworking - including the hidden paths – shows us not only what our barriers are but where they are as well. It brings them to the surface so that we must do something about them. This forces a reckoning that ultimately makes us more responsible and stronger. At the same time, it manifests wonderful rewards for us.

Hidden Paths from Malkuth

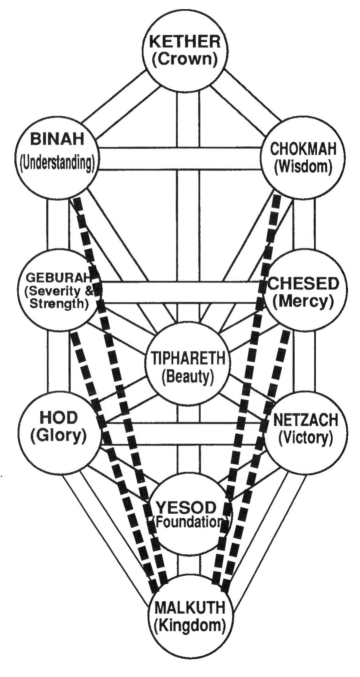

Malkuth to Geburah

Spiritual Experience:	Vision of the Gift of Life
Hidden Path Keynote:	Power to create and/or destroy
Divine Names:	Adonai ha Aretz / Elohim Gibor
Archangels:	Sandalphon and Kamael
Astrological Influences:	Earth & Mars / Pluto
Colors:	deep red or maroon; black
Magical gift/image:	flint, fire

Pathworking Benefits:
Creativity; strength to meet life's pressures; courage; fertility

Description:
This is a fiery path and the ancient myths of Vulcan reflect its qualities and lessons. This path stimulates the force of the ego. It will awaken a fighting spirit and reveal to us our ability to create and destroy. We feel a greater impulse to express ourselves in the external world. This path can be a tremendous tool for growth. It can help us destroy the old so that the new in us can be born.

With this path, the adage "Be careful what you ask for" could not be truer. Many ask for greater control over their life, and this path will open that up to us. And that is exciting. But it can also be a bit scary. If everything is now within our control, there will be no one to blame but ourselves if things do not work out the way we plan. With this path the universe tells us, "We are giving greater control of your life over to you. What you achieve or do not achieve will be entirely up to you, your own creativity and your own efforts. If you succeed the credit is all yours. If you fail, there is no one to blame but you."

Strengths Achieved:
Creativity; control over our life; strong creative impulse;

Weaknesses Revealed:
Selfishness, lust, impulsiveness, loss of control in our life; divisiveness; poor handling of life pressure

Malkuth to Chesed

Spiritual Experience:	Vision of Our Triumph
Hidden Path Keynote:	Power of compassion & wisdom
Divine Names:	Adonai ha Aretz / El
Archangels:	Sandalphon and Tzadkiel
Astrological Influences:	Earth & Jupiter
Colors:	deep blue-black indigo
Magical gift/image:	weather vane, kite

Pathworking Benefits:
Liberation; compassion; freedom from illusion; prophetic insights; wealth

Description:
In astrology, Jupiter is a planet that reflects when we triumph over the earth experience. This is a path that will help liberate us from personal considerations to more universal ones. It leads us away from personal goals to those of the community.

This path can open the gift of prophecy. We begin to see from where new winds are coming for us and our community. This is the path of the spiritual quest where wealth is discovered on many levels – mundane and spiritual. This path reveals the illusion of mundane wealth, while testing your ability to handle it appropriately.

This is a path of expansion. We begin to see that greater forces are at work in our life than we may have realized. This brings liberation from personal considerations. We begin to see universal laws operating and it initiates a change in our philosophy of life.

Strengths Achieved:
Prophecy; stronger sense of community; true wealth in life

Weaknesses Revealed:
Wandering spirit; always searching for something more; dissatisfaction

Malkuth to Binah

Spiritual Experience:	Vision of the Forces of Life
Hidden Path Keynote:	Open the Life (Akashic) Records
Divine Names:	Adonai ha Aretz / Jehovah Elohim
Archangels:	Sandalphon and Tzaphkiel
Astrological Influences:	Earth & Saturn
Colors:	black and olive
Magical gift/image:	clock (time), hour glass

Pathworking Benefits:
Learn to give; responsibility; revelation of Law of Karma in life

Description:
    This path crosses the abyss, affecting us on many more levels than we often discern. This is the path of karma and the play of light versus dark in our life. It will reveal why we have experienced some of the things we have in life. It can open the Akashic Records and bring understanding. We learn how the universal laws of life are playing out in our terrestrial existence. This path brings a reconciling of our human, material consciousness with the higher consciousness of our spirit. What can't be cured must be endured and this is part of what this hidden path reveals.

    This path teaches us how to mold the imagination to live successfully in the world. It shows us how we can be creative and pragmatic. It helps us find creative possibilities within our limitations. This hidden path helps us realize that the most spiritual act is the fulfilling of daily obligations and responsibilities. Sometimes we must step aside from formal spiritual studies to deal with life. But time is on our side. We can build an empire if we lay a strong foundation. Sometimes this means setting aside our personality for something greater.

Strengths Achieved:
Patience; faith; greater depth of imagination; understanding

Weaknesses Revealed:
Limitations and boundaries; impractical; selfishness; martyr

Malkuth to Chokmah

Spiritual Experience: Vision of the Divine in You
Hidden Path Keynote: Power of Inspiration
Divine Names: Adonai ha Aretz / Jah
Archangels: Sandalphon and Ratziel
Astrological Influences: Earth & Neptune
Colors: Deep, dark green
Magical gift/image: crystal ball,

Pathworking Benefits:
Purifying of visions and psychic abilities; self-sacrificing love, lucid and prophetic dreams

Description:
    This is a long path, extending from the bottom of the Tree to nearly the top. Longer paths are often more difficult, but the rewards are greater. The same is true for this path. It will set in motion the purifying of human consciousness on three levels – the physical body and senses, the astral and the emotions, and the mental body and our thoughts. And as a result our psychic vision and inspirational abilities are heightened beyond what we imagine.
    This is the path of the dreamer and the artist. It inspires creative imagination and true clairvoyant abilities. Our dreams will become more vivid – even lucid. And prophetic dreams begin to occur. This is a path though that will also force us to separate delusion from true vision – what really is as opposed to what we wish to see. It will help us distinguish between our fears and our realities.

Strengths Achieved:
Faith in visions; inspiration; creative imagination; artistic abilities

Weaknesses Revealed:
Laziness; delusion; deception; phobias

Hidden Paths from Yesod

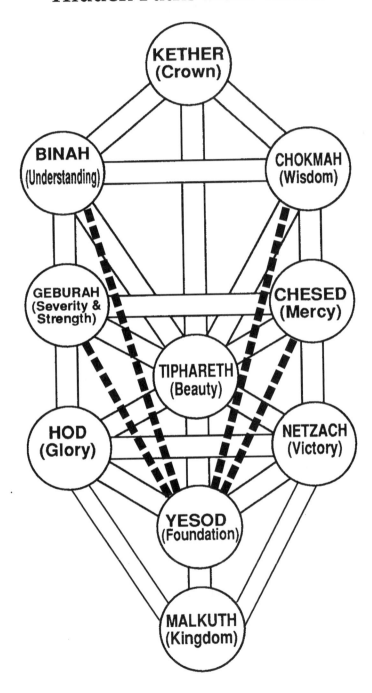

Yesod to Geburah

Spiritual Experience:	Vision of your role in the Divine Plan
Hidden Path Keynote:	Courage to live in the now
Divine Names:	Shaddai el Chai / Elohim Gibor
Archangels:	Gabriel and Kamael
Astrological Influences:	Moon & Mars / Pluto
Colors:	magenta
Magical gift/image:	candle; map

Pathworking Benefits:
Fertility; giving form to our dreams; increased ability to recognize opportunities; insight into the psyche of others

Description:
This path joins our feeling nature with our personal drives. In astrology, a conjunction of Moon and Mars will make the Moon's qualities more active. And through this pathworking, we find ourselves placed in a position of providing more light to others – reflecting our light out more strongly. Our instincts and emotions are bridged and given greater expression in the outer world.

This path will help us to recognize opportunities more quickly. It will help us to understand and make the best of situations. It awakens inner courage and self-confidence because we begin to learn that not only are we part of a Divine plan, but we also begin to discern our role in that plan more clearly. It gives us the opportunity to live in the now.

This path helps us recognize opportunities to act on our dreams. We discover that dreams are never lost – merely forgotten. We learn that we are never given a dream without also being given opportunities to make it a reality.

Strengths Achieved:
Fertility in endeavors; self-confidence; optimism; perceptiveness

Weaknesses Revealed:
Restlessness; lose sight of reality; anger and jealousy; procrastination; impulsiveness

Yesod to Chesed

Spiritual Experience:	Vision of the Love within
Hidden Path Keynote:	Power of hope
Divine Names:	Shaddai el Chai / El
Archangels:	Gabriel and Tzadkiel
Astrological Influences:	Moon & Jupiter
Colors:	deep blue-purple
Magical gift/image:	star, leather-bound volume

Pathworking Benefits:
Generosity; increased humor; more universal philosophy of life;

Description:
This is the path that expands our feelings from the self to the outer world. Love moves beyond love of self or one person to love of community to love of the world. This path opens us to give and receive helping hands into our life. It opens doors to self-exploration and higher knowledge so that we can begin to act, give initiative to our role in a more concrete form and expanded form. It thus becomes a path of generosity – an expression of the love within.

We find ourselves becoming more resourceful. We must face the fears we have about ourselves – along with our insecurities – and have hope that they are unfounded or can be overcome. Sometimes life brings upon us situations that must be looked at with humor – if only to keep our sanity. This path is a reminder to keep a sense of humor, maintain hope and keep our hearts open to others. As a result, we will succeed.

Strengths Achieved:
Happy-go-lucky; optimistic and hopeful; self-confidence;

Weaknesses Revealed:
False pride; insecurity; emotional uncertainty; restlessness

Yesod to Binah

Spiritual Experience:	Vision of Divine in the Mundane
Hidden Path Keynote:	Power of common sense
Divine Names:	Shaddai el Chai / Jehovah Elohim
Archangels:	Gabriel and Tzaphkiel
Astrological Influences:	Moon & Saturn
Colors:	charcoal gray (with a hint of violet)
Magical gift/image:	sash, abacus

Pathworking Benefits:

Endurance; increased perception; heightened sense of duty; blending of spiritual and physical in everyday life

Description:

People often talk about intuition being the sixth sense. In truth, common sense is the sixth. It is that part of us that is capable of taking what we have experienced through the five senses and synthesizes it into some kind of understanding. Once that is done, we are capable of making accurate intuitive leaps (seventh sense) from that point of understanding.

Binah can be the strict mother – the one who teaches the child (Yesod) what must be done to succeed in life. She helps develop abilities and apply them practically in life – including our psychic and intuitive abilities. One lesson in particular is that we have responsibilities and duties in life that must be fulfilled. This path helps us discern what our true responsibilities are and how to work with them for our greatest growth. This path helps us realize that everything we do in the mundane world is a miracle because we are spirit, simply housed in a physical body. And everything we do, learn and encounter is a wonder and an expression of the Divine.

Strengths Achieved:

Common sense; balanced practicality and intuition; ability to balance freedom and responsibility

Weaknesses Revealed:

Melancholy; cold hearted; irresponsible; selfishness

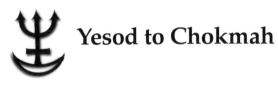 # Yesod to Chokmah

Spiritual Experience:	Vision of the Hidden Forces
Hidden Path Keynote:	Power to illuminate
Divine Names:	Shaddai el Chai / Jah
Archangels:	Sandalphon and Kamael
Astrological Influences:	Moon & Neptune
Colors:	gray and violet swirls
Magical gift/image:	owl

Pathworking Benefits:
Increased awareness of the spirit world; illumination surrounding events in our life; creative inspiration; uncovering secrets

Description:
This is the path of self-discovery. It helps us to recognize and understand hidden forces at play in our life and how to initiate our own hidden abilities. This is a path that reveals the illusions of our life. These may be illusions that we have created around ourselves and illusions that have been created around us by outside entities – people in our life, society, etc.

This is a path that can help you discover hidden activities around you. If you have been suspecting or perceiving undercurrents (being lied to or misled or suspecting secrets about you), then this path will stimulate a play of events in your life that will bring them to light. You will soon know one way or the other. This path stirs our creative and artistic energies. We begin to find new inspiration and illumination around us. New opportunities arise for greater self-expression. It will awaken a greater openness to life.

Strengths Achieved:
Discrimination and discernment; openness to life experiences; artistic expression

Weaknesses Revealed:
Inability to separate real from unreal; moodiness; deception

Hidden Paths from Hod & Netzach

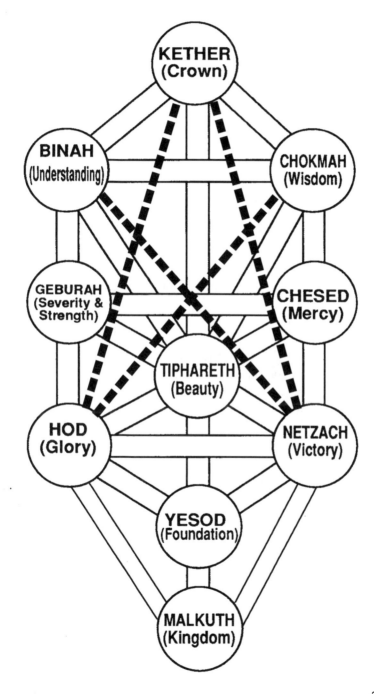

 # Hod to Chokmah

Spiritual Experience:	Vision of Truth
Hidden Path Keynote:	Power of keen observation/ perception
Divine Names:	Elohim Tzabaoth/ Jah
Archangels:	Michael and Ratziel
Astrological Influences:	Mercury & Neptune
Colors:	silvery gray
Magical gift/image:	quill pen, paint brush

Pathworking Benefits:
Discernment of truth; artistic and creative energies; empowered communication; lucid dreaming

Description:
    This path is one of the most beneficial for opening up and removing artistic blocks. For those with writer's block or who might feel restricted in expressing their creative and artistic abilities, this path will help. It will release energies in your life that will create opportunities to express yourself more artistically.

    This path awakens the poetic and artistic mind and helps reveal the truth of our own creativity. It will reveal where lack of concentration and focus may be hindering you in your expressions. Our dreams will become more lucid and our intuition is much more highly sensitive. We become aware that anything is possible.

    This path brings balance between logic and intuition, heightening both within us. This combination that allows us to see the truth of people and situations around us. It will manifest situations that will help us recognize what is real in our life and that what isn't – the truth as opposed to falsehoods. When we know the truth, harmony is restored in and around us.

Strengths Achieved:
Harmony; focus; rich imagination; acceptance of others

Weaknesses Revealed:
Fault-finding; deception; untruthfulness; lack of concentration

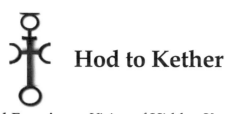 # Hod to Kether

Spiritual Experience: Vision of Hidden Knowledge
Hidden Path Keynote: Power to awaken the unconscious mind
Divine Names: Elohim Tzabaoth / Eheieh
Archangels: Michael and Metatron
Astrological Influences: Mercury and Uranus
Colors: electric blue
Magical gift/ image: lighthouse, spark

Pathworking Benefits:
Self-reliance; knowledge of past lives; sparks of genius; progressive thinking

Description:
 This is a path of action. It stimulates tremendous inventiveness. The originality can take on the spark of genius. This is a path of intuitive communication from deep within the subconscious mind to the outer conscious ness.

 This path will stimulate opportunities to see both sides of issues and create opportunity to put words into action. This path will teach you that it is not what you say that is most important but rather how you say it.

 This is the path of the disciplined mind through which many wonders become possible – including tapping into past life knowledge and their play upon the present life circumstances. It is the disciplined and open mind that allows us to probe the unconscious and bring forth new insights and to give birth to new ideas.

Strengths Achieved:
Inventiveness; lightning mind; self-reliance; focus

Weaknesses Revealed:
Jumps to conclusions; tendency to disbelieve; scattered thinking

Netzach to Binah

Spiritual Experience:	Vision of Creation
Hidden Path Keynote:	Power to give birth and share
Divine Names:	Jehovah Tzabaoth / Jehovah Elohim
Archangels:	Haniel and Tzaphkiel
Astrological Influences:	Venus and Saturn
Colors:	dark, olive green
Magical gift/ image:	sea shells, whale, butterfly

Pathworking Benefits:
Creative and spiritual power of sexuality; personal magnetism; the power of sharing; deep compassion (especially for Nature)

Description:
This is the path of primal Nature. Nature is the most powerful realm of magic and spirituality available to us. It is a source of great primal energies and spirits. It contains most of life's lessons. Life, death and rebirth play out continually within it. This path opens us to those same primal energies. We learn about our own innate ability to give birth – whether we are male or female. Binah can reflect the crone or old wise woman and Netzach can reflect the mother or maiden, so in this path we have two aspects of the divine feminine at play – so often reflected and revealed within Nature.

This path opens us to love, compassion, sex and wisdom and reveals where and how we are using or misusing these energies in our life. It will open us to emotional involvements while revealing where such involvements are not healthy. It can also strengthen our innate connection to Nature and her spirits.

Strengths Achieved:
Patience; ability to share more deeply; compassion; sense of duty to loved ones; trust in ability to create

Weaknesses Revealed:
Impatience; irresponsibility; restraint; manipulation; coldness in relationships

256

Netzach to Kether

Spiritual Experience: Vision of primordial life
Hidden Path Keynote: Power of sexuality
Divine Names: Jehovah Tzabaoth / Eheieh
Archangels: Haniel and Metatron
Astrological Influences: Venus and Uranus
Colors: emerald
Magical gift/image: dolphin/ tree in the spring

Pathworking Benefits:
Creative epiphanies; strong personal magnetism; dynamic intuition; animal communication

Description:
     This is the path of primordial beginnings – when the first seeds of life began to form. It is a path of active creativity – of accelerated birth and growth. It is the path of innate connection to the natural world.

     It is the path of sexuality – physical and spiritual. Sex is one of the great mysteries of life. When the male and female are brought together in any form, a birth will occur. When the male and female come together within us – the Holy Child Within is born. When we learn to take our innate creativity (Netzach) and give it dynamic impulse (Kether), we are changed.

     This is the path of the dreamer, the mystic, the poet and the holy child. It can stir many latent creative talents. Finding that balance without becoming lost in inappropriate expressions of our creativity (sexual energies) is often tested and revealed through this pathworking. At the very least, it awakens our originality and creates new values. You become more powerful in the unconventional.

Strengths Achieved:
Intense expression; balanced love and freedom; live in the now

Weaknesses Revealed:
Unusual, unbalanced behaviors; inappropriate sexual activities; emotional ups and downs

Hidden Paths from Chesed & Geburah

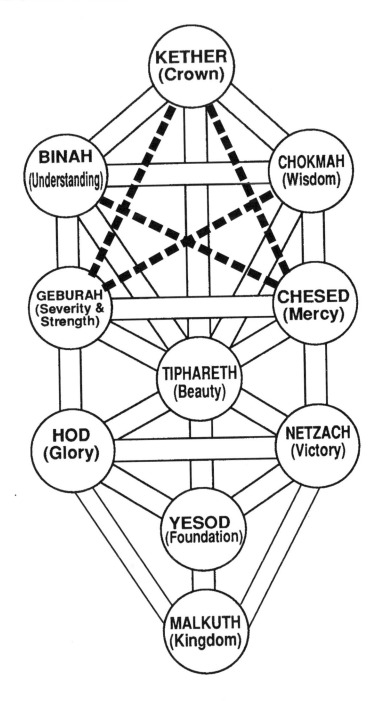

Geburah to Chokmah

Spiritual Experience: Vision of Wisdom
Hidden Path Keynote: Power to lead
Divine Names: Elohim Gibor / Jah
Archangels: Kamael and Ratziel
Astrological Influences: Mars and Neptune
Colors: gray and maroon
Magical gift/image: hawk, arrow

Pathworking Benefits:
Patiently guide; practical idealist; opportunity and ability to take charge; others recognize your leadership

Description:
    This is a path that begins immediately in the Abyss that separates the lower seven sephiroth from the three upper or supernal sephiroth. The Abyss is an area of fog and illusion and thus a strong leader is required to truly guide others across. This path will bring to light your own leadership abilities or lack of them.

    This is the Hero's path. Hero's often undertake quests and experience great heights of glory and great depths of despair. This is a Karmic path that tests your ability to lovingly assert and guide without discouraging those that look to you for that guidance.

    In many ways, this is a path of learning to go forward in faith – trusting in the innocent wisdom that lies deep within you (sometimes called the Fool's Wisdom). It helps us realize that we have much more power and wisdom over our life circumstances than we may realize.

Strengths Achieved:
Courage; ambition; patiently assertive; consistent and decisive

Weaknesses Revealed:
Insensitivity; bullying; restlessness; discouraging; obsessive

Geburah to Kether

Spiritual Experience:	Vision of True Spiritual Power
Hidden Path Keynote:	Ability to overcome
Divine Names:	Elohim Gibor / Eheieh
Archangels:	Kamael and Metatron
Astrological Influences:	Mars and Uranus
Colors:	scarlet
Magical gift/image:	vulture, journey staff

Pathworking Benefits:
Vitality; overcoming difficulties; foresight; order from chaos

Description:
    This is another of those paths which start directly in the Abyss. This is a path that will stir up what needs to be controlled and straightened out in your life. You will likely have to face your fears, doubts, limitations and things in your life that have been creating chaos or disruption on some level. Remember that Qabalistic pathworking - including the hidden paths – shows us not only what our barriers are but where they are as well. It brings them to the surface, forcing a reckoning that ultimately makes us more responsible and stronger. At the same time, it manifests wonderful rewards for us. This is a path that brings this process into manifestation very clearly.
    This volatile path will bring opportunities to overcome difficulties. If you are patient you will progress and do so effectively. As a result you will stand out from the crowd as a peacemaker and strong. It will require though that we think before acting, and be persistent. We must trust our intuition in devising the best plan to work for the individual situations, even if it means opposing the status quo.

Strengths Achieved:
Decisiveness; courage; persistence; foresight; discipline

Weaknesses Revealed:
Difficulty taking instruction; erratic behavior; impulsiveness

Chesed to Binah

Spiritual Experience:	Vision of the Infinite
Hidden Path Keynote:	Power to create prosperity
Divine Names:	El / Jehovah Elohim
Archangels:	Tzadkiel and Tzaphkiel
Astrological Influences:	Jupiter and Saturn
Colors:	Rich, dark indigo
Magical gift:	treasure chest, cornucopia, bison

Pathworking Benefits:

Prosperity; idealism; ability to achieve; expansion of wealth (mundane and spiritual); good fortune

Description:

This is the path that opens the flow of rewards for our efforts. It reminds us that if we put right effort with right thought, we will succeed. More importantly, it is a reminder that there is abundance in the Universe and as sons and daughters of the Divine we are the inheritors of that abundance.

The laws of prosperity operate for everyone, but we must be willing to receive. Shortly after performing this pathworking, pay close attention to what is offered to you. If someone pays you a compliment, accept it graciously. If someone offers to give you something, accept it joyfully. If someone offers you help, accept it gratefully. If we do not accept the little things, the universe will not give us the big things. We must realize that our spirit is deserving of abundance. This path shows us that we have the ability to achieve any objective through patience and perseverance. This is a path that will help to awaken good fortune or to face those things that may be preventing.

Strengths Achieved:

Discipline; patience; idealism; ability to follow through

Weaknesses Revealed:

Inability to follow through; impatience; contradictory feelings about our worth; inertia; blame

Chesed to Kether

Spiritual Experience:	Vision of Holy Quest
Hidden Path Keynote:	Power to
Divine Names:	El / Eheieh
Archangels:	Tzadkiel and Metatron
Astrological Influences:	Jupiter and Uranus
Colors:	steel blue and gold
Magical gift/image:	king's cup, grail

Pathworking Benefits:
Opens the spiritual quest; strengthens intuitive judgment; awakens thirst for knowledge; manifests new experiences

Description:
This is the path of adventure. It stimulates a thirst for knowledge, for exploring and for our own spiritual quest. The spiritual quest though is to find the light within us, so that we can shine it out. This path will bring opportunities to clarify our current path in life and how aligned it is or is not with our true desires – our true spiritual quest. Are we pursuing our dreams? What do we need to do to shift to a more fulfilling life path? Working this path will bring upon you situations that will force you to examine these questions, but it will also open doors for changes – if that is what you truly wish.

This is the path that tests your judgment in regards to your path in life. It can bring good fortune and open doors, but you must be willing to accept it and walk through those doors, leaving old paths behind. This path brings opportunities for transformation and changes in life direction – revealing possibilities that wait for those who pursue with wisdom.

Strengths Achieved:
Keen judgment; clear intuition; optimism; tolerance of others

Weaknesses Revealed:
Insecure; dogmatic and afraid of anything new; dissatisfaction; fear of change; issues of alone versus lonely

Important Note

All pathworkings have a guardian aspect for security, safety and balance. These are primarily divine names, the archangelic energies and the path symbol. The divine names will dissolve any inappropriate energies and images. The path symbol will provide for you an emergency exit. Simply visualize a door around it that opens into the temple where the journey began. It is also good to visualize yourself in the company of the archangel of the temple you begin with.

All meditations, journeys and pathworkings have a beginning, middle and end. Most will begin inside the Tree where the temple of origin is found most easily. This temple is one step removed from our day-to-day consciousness and life. If our work or exercise is interrupted, simply visualize the temple of origin. From it you can easily step from the Tree, and you will be brought back to your normal state of consciousness - safely.

Every path contains milestones or markers to help you identify the right path once you have started. This is why previewing the symbols and images of the paths helps. If you do not see them in any form along the path, or if the path changes color, it usually indicates that you have wandered off track. Return your focus by visualizing the path in the appropriate color. This will keep you on track. If that becomes difficult, focus on the Temple of origin, return to it, and exit the Tree. It may be that this is not the time to attempt that particular path.

It is good to plan on seeing the symbols of the path somewhere along the path itself. It is easy to do, especially if you use the methods of creating the pathworking scenarios yourself. These are described later in this chapter. The symbols are the key to a successful pathworking. They relate to the energies of the path itself and they serve as a catalyst for the archetypal forces. They keep us connected to those spiritually subtle energies of the path.

There may arise a time along the path when you feel you cannot complete the working. Maybe you are uncomfortable with the energies. Maybe you are feeling a little fearful or doubtful. Do not be upset by this! *And above all, honor that!* Ultimately you know what you can handle and at what rate. There is no sense in traumatizing yourself. It won't help you grow any more.

Simply visualize the temple of origin, and allow yourself to return to it. Then exit the Tree. Work on the sephiroth or other paths until you feel comfortable working the one that created the distress. Emotional upset can occur during a pathworking, and although it often reflects that we have successfully accessed the archetypal forces there, part of our development requires that we honor ourselves by not traumatizing ourselves in the growing process.

Some of the pathworkings will have immediate effects upon your life. Others may take weeks or even months before their manifestation and impacts will be fully recognized. *Be assured, they will have an impact. They will affect your life on all levels.*

Initiation involves change and growth. Through pathworking, we hasten that process. The phrase, "Be careful what you ask for because you may receive it" is quite appropriate. When you work with the Qabala and magical pathworking, you are asking for a complete awakening - not just enough to satisfy curiosity or a need for psychic thrills. The energy released and its effects are often stronger than we imagined.

Some of the more abstract paths and levels can be the most powerful and the most effective. Some that we would expect to have the least impact may have the most. Not everyone will be affected the same way. We each are progressing and developing in our own unique manner. The energy released will play within our lives in a unique manner. But every word, phrase and picture can trigger chain reactions which rise to the surface within our life.

There is freedom within the paths and the visual

images created through the workings. This is why the most powerful and effective pathworkings are those in which we create the scenario in accordance with the energies and symbols of the path itself. This technique is described later in this chapter, and through it the archetypal energies will play more dynamically and uniquely within our lives. This is what makes it such an individual and yet vital growth process. It will amplify the effects.

Most importantly, do not make the mistake of thinking that these techniques are an excuse for daydreaming and psychic thrill-seeking! They are so much more than mere fantasy, and such assumptions will be devastated by the truth of their power being driven home!

Glyphs of the Hidden Paths

The glyphs shown with each of the hidden path descriptions are powerfully effective for opening the doors to that hidden paths and to its energies. I have used them for years with tremendous success.

Exercise

Temple to Temple Visitations

Benefits:

- **guidance on your pathworking**
- **facilitates the process of pathworking**
- **helps in understanding**

Each sephira is actually a temple of consciousness in which our more universal capacities reside. In this magical pathworking, we use these temples of the mind as starting points and destinations, thereby bridging the energies of two levels of consciousness more strongly.

In the past we learned to activate different levels of consciousness for greater *illumination*. We are now linking the levels that will release the energies and manifest conditions for *initiation*. We will manifest situations that will help us to apply that illumination more fully within our life.

We always start by entering the Tree of Life. Once inside, we awaken the temple, as we learned earlier in the book. Then we create a doorway behind the altar that opens to the path that leads to the next temple. For the hidden paths, use the glyph for the path that I have provided. I have used them for years with great success and benefit. Visualize the glyph engraved into the door. Trace it with your finger and as you do, have the door open. Through the open door, you can see the path leading out from it and the distant temple.

Sometimes with the hidden paths, the second temple is not visible. As you move along the path, occasionally tone the divine names for both temples. This will provide protection and prevent you from getting lost.

Through the doorway, we step out onto a path of the appropriate color, leading to the second temple. As we step onto the path, we are met by the archangels of the two sephiroth. We may choose to be met by the magical images as well or instead of. These are our escorts. As you walk along the path, discuss with your escorts the purpose and function of the path and how its energies are likely to manifest within your life.

Along the way, various things may be encountered. These will vary somewhat from individual to individual, but the things encountered are markers that let you know that you have not wandered off the path. **THIS IS IMPORTANT!** We need the markers. On some paths there may be no companions. We may need to walk them alone - experiencing and synthesizing the energies for ourselves. Often in such cases, the archangelic influence may not appear until the destination is reached.

These markers should be planned for ahead of the actual working. If they are not seen, then it is important that we visualize them into being. By doing so, we link ourselves back to the path if we have wandered. If we have not, it serves to make our connection to the path stronger.

The first marker is the **color of the path.** No matter how long the journey may seem, as long as you stay on the path of the appropriate color, we will ultimately reach our destination. I often visualize myself, dressed in the colors of the path with my clothing trimmed in the colors of the two sephiroth. It's just an added precaution.

Plan to encounter **a road mark** of some sort approximately halfway through the pathworking. This is the second marker. The road sign or marker should have the symbol for the path on it as well. This helps activate the energies and anchors us more strongly to that specific pathworking. It helps keep us from getting lost. I sometimes visualize a necklace with a medallion hanging from a tree, halfway through the working. Engraved into the medallion is one of the symbols for the particular path I am working. With the hidden paths, I use the symbol depicted with the hidden path descriptions. Sometimes I also visualize the gifts of the path, waiting for me at the halfway point.

Individuals other than your guides and escorts may appear upon the path. The more you learn about the path and its energies, the more significant they will become. There are many symbols and images that reflect the forces of the path. With time and practice, you will learn to recognize when others that show up have something to do with the path itself.

Usually, the individuals that are appropriate to the path will have insignias of the path on them when you are working the traditional paths. Often times the insignias are the Hebrew letter or the astrological glyph. It may appear as an insignia upon the individual's attire or even upon the individual's body - such as a tattoo. It is not always as clear when working the hidden paths, so if you are unsure, leave the person alone and continue on to the second temple, gathering your gifts along the way.

When you step into the second temple, call it into being, using the Divine name for the temple. Visualize it in as much detail as possible, with all of its appropriate colors and symbols. Allow the archangel to greet you. Thank the Archangel for the protection and guidance on this working.

Now it is time to close the temple and bring the gifts out into your real life. The easiest way to do this is by alternating the toning of the Divine names of the two temples. Slowly tone or speak the Divine name of the first temple, followed by the Divine name for the second. Repeat this for a total of three times. With each repetition, see, feel and imagine the temple fading from the inner vision to be born into your outer life.

Take a few minutes to quietly reflect on the path and the meaning of the gifts as they are likely to unfold into your daily life circumstances.

Conclusion

Human Becoming

The qualities essential for accelerating our growth and spiritual evolution are innate, although this idea is often unrecognized or believed to be only for the realm of the gifted few. Even when this innate ability is recognized though, there is still needed an effective system or a means to release it. In our modern world, there are a myriad of individuals providing maps. How then are we to know which map to follow through the labyrinth of spiritual explorations?

The key is to remember that ultimately no one knows better for us than ourselves, and there is no one doing anything in the spiritual and metaphysical realm that we cannot also be doing in our own unique way. We must learn to take what we can from whatever source we can, work with it and adapt it into a method that works for us as individuals.

Then whatever system we use as a guide to explore other realms inside or outside of us should fulfill certain criteria. Such a system should be easily understood, and if based upon an older Mystery Tradition, it should be living and growing, adaptable to the modern world and to us within it. The system should be capable of awakening our inner potentials without overwhelming us in the process. Finally, it should enable us to experience the universal energies that fill and touch our lives daily.

The ancient mystical Qabala fulfills all of these

criteria. It is a map that allows us to look into ourselves for our answers, for our magic and for our miracles. Not from books or from teachers - although they serve their purposes - but from the well of truth that lies within! Rather than searching for some light to shine down upon us, the Qabala guides us to the light within - to shine out from us! Only then does the path through the labyrinth of life become a path to the Holy Grail.

There will be those who say that hidden paths do not exist in traditional Qabala. And that is true. But if Qabala is to remain a truly living system of spiritual development and unfoldment, we must build upon its foundation and find new expressions of it. It does not lessen it. In fact, it reveals even more greatness to it as a system of higher initiation.

All of the methods in this book deal with learning to open the doors that are closed. It does not matter who closed them; what is important is that we allowed them to be closed. We each have the ability to open the doors that will shed light into the dark corners of our life. In this way, we see exactly what needs to be cleaned. And we discover what potentials lie hidden within us.

Much has been written about meditation and its various practices. There are, in fact, as many methods of meditation as there are people. As to which method or combination of methods is best, no one can answer that but the individual. What is important is that the method chosen be an active one. It is not enough to simply quiet the mind and allow pleasant images to arise. Over time, this can lead to self-deception. We need to act upon what we are stimulating. We operate predominantly within the physical dimension, and thus all energies activated on other levels need to be grounded into the physical.

The techniques in this book are not truly magical. They may seem so to the uninformed, but they are simply techniques for developing our innate potentials. They help us to solve problems, achieve goals, open ourselves to higher capabilities and re-instill color and a joy of life. Their application to daily life is work, as any active form of development is. That work though can be enjoyable. As it is often said, it is not the destination, but the journey itself that holds the treasures. If we are to maximize the effects of our work, we must actively use whatever knowledge, inspiration and awareness within our daily lives.

There are quick methods to open our psychic energies, but they alone do not propel us along our spiritual path to a higher destiny. Neither do they reflect a higher evolution. Only by bridging the psychic with the spiritual archetypes and then grounding them into the physical do we create opportunities for higher evolution.

Many wish to open doors because of a power they hope to demonstrate. This, in and of itself, is not wrong, but it is limiting. It is also a natural by-product of opening and clearing the bridges between the levels of consciousness. Our powers unfold naturally as we grow in knowledge and experience, and they can be developed by anyone. But it does not reflect any higher evolution or a more moral or spiritual character.

The entire purpose of working with Tree of Life and the techniques within this book or my previous books on Qabala is to increase our awareness of the interplay of other dimensions with our physical life so we can learn to control them. This involves removing tunnel vision approach to life and overcoming reliance only upon the five senses. We must learn to use altered states of consciousness to recognize and understand how energies play upon us in all aspects of our life. We must learn to synthesize the inner realm experiences with the outer reality.

Through pathworking, we can look at the patterns of our lives. We begin with the inherent capabilities and our present proficiency with them. We must look for the patterns and relationships between our lives and the lives of others. Are we repeating the same situations and experiences? We must retrain ourselves to look at life and people from all levels.

Working with the Tree of Life means opening up the intuition and ability to perceive our life in new dimensions. We will no longer be able to perceive people and things from a limited, physical perspective. Everything is affected by us, and everything affects us. Control of our environment begins with control of our self. Until we cease to be influenced haphazardly by surrounding conditions, we cannot hope to exercise influence over them.

This means that we must learn to grow and extend ourselves in an environment that promotes growth and provides protection. Through the Qabalistic Tree of Life, we achieve both. This book provides tools and techniques that will aid our growth. They will assist your unfolding and provide protection for you as we open to new potentials and new dimensions.

The Great Work

When working with the Tree of Life, we are trying to bridge our spiritual essence to our physical being, so that we can access it consciously at any time we desire for any purpose we desire. When we make efforts to raise our consciousness, we stimulate the release of energy from our spiritual essence to be expressed within the physical life. By working with the Tree of Life we are learning to consciously stimulate the release of energy and to direct its flow and expression into our daily lives. This energy, once released, must find expression. That expression can be beneficial or detrimental because energy is neutral - neither good nor evil. It is only our expression and use of it that determines it.

That expression may become disruptive and destructive, finding inappropriate outlets in the physical life if there are not proper mental, emotional and moral foundations. It can over stimulate the individual in a variety of ways, affecting physical, emotional, and mental health and balance. If not prepared for, it will often find outlet through the person's own weaknesses, augmenting them and bringing them out into the open.

Because of the amount of information and knowledge available today, we do not always need a teacher to open to the more subtle realms of life. Methods and means of doing so can be found everywhere. The problem lies in assuming that the knowledge and information is true and safe. There is a great abundance of information available, but much of it is very irresponsible, and so the spiritual student must be even more discerning and discriminating. This is the spiritual lesson of Malkuth. It is the first thing we must learn and the last thing we will be tested upon on the spiritual path.

Because of the predominance of information, most people will not align themselves with truly qualified teachers, and this more solitary approach requires even greater personal responsibility. The student of the mysteries must still earn the conditions necessary for higher initiation and consciousness. This requires even greater time, care and responsibility in the development process.

There is no fast and easy way. Having done so in a past life does not override the training necessary in this life and those who teach or profess such are living an illusion. We may have learned to read in a previous life or even ten, but we still had to relearn it in this life. We had to learn the alphabet, the phonics, develop a vocabulary and so on. We must be cautious of our assumptions drawn from misinformation, half-truths and incomplete knowledge.

Today, the spiritual path demands a *fully* conscious union with the spiritually creative worlds. This cannot be accomplished by mere clairvoyance or psychism of any kind. Today's path to manifesting a higher destiny requires a genuine search and use of knowledge and truth. It requires a greater depth of study of all spiritual sciences. It requires remembering that information and knowledge is not always truthful and will not always benefit.

We live in a fast food society. People like to pull up to the drive through window, get their food and drive on. They look for the quick and the easy, even with the spiritual. Many spiritual students want to pull up to the drive through window, get their psychic stuff and then drive on as well. No effort, no work, no problems.

Unfortunately, many spiritual, magical and new age aspirants attempt to *be* before they have learned to *become*. It always trips them up through a variety of imbalances. So often people tell me, "You know, I had this great vision and I acted on it, and things started out wonderfully. Then it all changed and everything went wrong." There is an old Qabalistic adage: *A vision of God is not the same as seeing God face to face.* In other words, a vision is not a promise of what will be. It is a reflection of what can be if there is the proper preparation, knowledge and application of focus, energy and persistence.

Yes, there are quick ways of "rending the veils" - to open to forces and dimensions more subtle, but if the personal wires cannot carry the load, the current will become distorted or closed. It will burn itself up. It is dangerous to enter the spiritual, more subtle realms of life and energy with a thinking that has only been strengthened through meditation, gathering information or mere psychic development. There needs to be an in-depth study and knowledge of the entire path of esoteric schooling in order to truly heal and intensify soul activities and to balance the events of one's life and align it with the universal process. It is to aid in this that Daath, the second secret door, reveals its importance in the modern Qabala.

Frequently those with just a little knowledge feel they are constantly in control when in reality they are not. Unfortunately, the true realization of not being in control does not occur until it is usually too late. Even if techniques have been learned in previous lives - which many psychics and modern day pseudo-mystics credit for their facility - it still requires proper training to awaken the potentials in the safest most beneficial manner.

Our mind is a gateway to other dimensions. It has been said that we enter the mysteries through the sphere of the mind but only so we can worship at the shrine in the heart. Humans have grown increasingly rational in our thinking processes during this past century, and often this colors our higher feeling aspects. Today we need to link the mind with the heart and with the often hidden soul.

The true spiritual student should be familiar with the spiritual investigations and philosophies of the past. There must be the ability for complete and independent testing of the knowledge. The individual needs to develop the ability to draw correspondences and see relationships - similar and dissimilar. He or she must be able to discern truth from half-truth and illusions from reality.

There are no shortcuts. Through the Tree of Life though, we learn to open to higher knowledge and hidden potential. We learn to use them to integrate the spiritual forces surrounding us into our daily lives in a balanced fashion.

This doesn't mean it will be easy. It just means that now we have a great tool to help us. It means we can learn to invoke and invite energies into our lives that can bring results. It requires great time and effort, but it also brings great rewards for that time and effort.

A great secret lesson of knowledge is that nothing is insignificant. Everything has importance and consequence within our lives, helping to shape us. Recognizing this is what working with the Tree of Life is all about. Learning to utilize and incorporate all of our energies at all times – visible and hidden, in full consciousness and with full responsibility - is the Great Work. It is *becoming* more than human; it is what makes us a human *being.*

Conclusion

Appendix

Pronunciation Guide

The guide that follows is to help provide a basis of correct pronunciation for the Hebrew words and names used most frequently with the Qabala. For our purposes, we will focus on the pronunciations for the sephiroth, their corresponding divine names and the archangelic names as well.

There are, of course, dialectical differences that do exist, but it is important not to become hung up on that aspect. If one is close in pronunciation, and focuses upon its correlations, the energies will be activated.

The names are spelled out phonetically, using the more common phonetic pronunciations found within any American dictionary. For the most part, several points should be kept in mind. (If some of these seem too obvious, and I imagine some people may roll their eyes at parts of this guideline, please be patient. I receive a great deal of mail and I am frequently asked questions about the proper pronunciations, in spite of phonetic spellings provided in my earlier texts.)

1. There are no vowels in the Hebrew alphabet. Vowel sounds are designated by diacritical marks. I have provided English phonetics for these sounds that are as close to the Hebrew pronunciations as possible.

2. In general, our consonant sounds are very similar or identical to the Hebrew, and so the consonant sounds should be pronounced as you would in English.

3. There are, of course, always exceptions. For example, the English language has no sound that is equivalent to the Hebrew "cheth" or "ch" sound. For those with a familiarity with the German language, the "ch" is pronounced a lot like the German words "nicht" or "ich". (Some people compare this to a soft clearing of the throat.) Until you become practiced in the more guttural pronunciation, pronouncing it as our traditional "k" sound will work quite well.

4. Long vowel sounds (where the vowel speaks its own name) are reflected through being written in capital letters. Thus an "E" is pronounced as in the word *bee.*

5. For vowels that are pronounced like the long sound of another vowel, it will be spelled out in capitals of the vowel whose sound it has. For example, for the sephira Binah the "i" has a long E (as in bee) sound. Thus it is spelled out phonetically as "bE - nah".

6. Short vowel sounds, are spelled phonetically, and with the key provided, there should be little confusion.

7. Although, most Hebrew words have an accent on the last syllable, for the basis of our work with the Qabala, give each syllable equal length and accent.

In the guide that follows, the information is in no way complete. Generalizations are made, and some of the more subtle distinctions in pronunciation have been eliminated. For example, the difference in pronunciation between the "t" of tau and the "t" of teth" is not distinguished and is rarely recognized by anyone other than those who are extremely familiar with the Hebrew tongue and language. These generalizations will not diminish your effectiveness and power when intoning these names.

VOWELS   PRONUNCIATIONS

(REMEMBER: The long sounding vowels are designated and written with a capital letter. The short sounding vowels are spelled phonetically and will not be capitalized throughout this guide.)

a	"ah" sound as in *father*
	"uh" sound as in *sofa*
e	"eh" sound as in *bet*
	"E" sound as in *bee*
	"A" sound as in hay
i	"ih" sound as in *bit*
	"E" sound as in *bee*
	"I" sound as in *bite*
o	"ah" sound as in *not*
	"O" sound as in *opal*
u	"uh" sound as in *but*
	"U" sound as in *you*
ai	"I" as in *bite*

SEPHIROTH   PRONUNCIATION

Sephiroth	Pronunciation
Malkuth	mahl - kUth
Yesod	yeh-sahd
Hod	hOd
Netzach	neht-zahk
Tiphareth	tih-fah-rehth
Geburah	geh-bU-rah
Chesed	heh-sehd
Binah	bE-nah
Chokmah	hahk-mah
Kether	keh-thehr

SEPHIRA	DIVINE NAME	PRONUNCIATION
Malkuth	Adonai ha Aretz	ah-DO-nI-hah-ah-rehtz
Yesod	Shaddai El Chai	shah-dI-ehl-kI
Hod	Elohim Tzabaoth	eh-lO-hEm-tzah-bah-Oth
Netzach	Jehovah Tzabaoth	yah-hO-vah-tzah-bah-Oth
Tiphareth	Jehovah Aloah va Daath	yah-hO-vah-A-lO-ah-vuh-dahth
Geburah	Elohim Gibor	A-lO-hEm-gih-bOr
Chesed	El	ehl
Binah	Jehovah Elohim	yah-hO-vah-A-lO-hEm
Chokmah	Jah	yah
Kether	Eheieh	A-huh-yAh

SEPHIRA	ARCHANGEL	PRONUNCIATION
Malkuth	Sandalphon	sahn-dahl-fOn
Yesod	Gabriel	gah-brE-ehl
Hod	Michael	mE-kah-ehl
Netzach	Haniel	hah-nI-ehl
Tiphareth	Raphael	rah-fah-ehl
Geburah	Kamael	kah-mah-ehl
Chesed	Tzadkiel	zahd-kI-ehl
Binah	Tzaphkiel	zahf-kI-ehl
Chokmah	Ratziel	raht-zI-ehl
Kether	Metatron	meh-tuh-trOn

Bibliography

Andrews, Ted. *SIMPLIFIED MAGIC.* Llewellyn Publications; St. Paul, 1989.

_____. *MORE SIMPLIFIED MAGIC.* Dragonhawk Publishing. Jackson, TN. 1998.

_____. *HOW TO HEAL WITH COLOR.* Llewellyn Publications; St. Paul, 1992.

_____. *SACRED SOUNDS.* Llewellyn Publications; St. Paul, 1992.

_____. *ANIMAL-SPEAK.* Llewellyn Publications; St. Paul, 1993.

_____. *MAGICKAL DANCE.* Llewellyn Publications; St. Paul, 1992.

_____. *NATURE-SPEAK.* Dragonhawk Publishing. Jackson, TN; 2004.

_____. *THE ART OF SHAPESHIFTING.* Dragonhawk Publishing. Jackson, TN; 2005

Ashcroft-Nowicke, Dolores. *THE SHINING PATHS.* Aquarian Press; Northamptonshire,1983.

Brennon, J.H. *ASTRAL DOORWAYS.* Aquarian Press; Northamptonshire, 1986.

Cooper, J.C. *SYMBOLISM - The Universal Language.* Aquarian Press; Northamptonshire, 1982.

Fortune, Dion. *THE MYSTICAL QABALA.* Ernst Benn Limited; London, 1979.

_____. *ASPECTS OF OCCULTISM.* Aquarian Press; Northamptonshire, 1986.

_____. *PRACTICAL OCCULTISM IN DAILY LIFE.* Aquarian Press; Northamptonshire, 1981.

Godwin, David. *CABALISTIC ENCYCLOPEDIA.* Llewellyn Publications; St. Paul, 1989.

Halevi, Z'ev ben Shimon. *ADAM AND THE KABBALISTIC TREE.* Weiser Publishing; York Beach, 1985.

Hall, Manly P. *MAN - GRAND SYMBOL OF THE MYSTERIES.* Philosophical Research Society; Los Angeles, 1972.

_____. *SECRET TEACHINGS OF THE AGES.* Philosophical
Research Society; Los Angeles, 1977.

Jung, Carl. *ARCHETYPES AND THE GREAT UNCONSCIOUS.*
_____. *THE COLLECTED WORKS (Vol. 18).* Princeton University
Press; Princeton, 1976.

Knight, Gareth. *PRACTICAL GUIDE TO QABALISTIC SYMBOLISM.*
Weiser Publishing; York Beach, 1978.

Steiner, Rudolph. *AN OUTLINE OF OCCULT SCIENCE.*
Anthroposophical Press; Hudson, 1972.
_____. *KNOWLEDGE OF THE HIGHER WORLDS.*
Anthroposophical Press; Hudson, 1947.
_____. *SPIRITUAL HIERARCHIES.* Anthroposophical Press;
Hudson, 1970

Waite, A.E. *THE HOLY KABBALAH.* University Books/ Citadel Press,
Secaucus.

Weinstein, Marion. *POSITIVE MAGIC.* Phoenix Publishing; Boulder,
1978.

Wippler, Migene Gonzales. *A KABBALAH FOR THE MODERN
WORLD.* Llewellyn Publications; St. Paul, 1987.

Index

More Simplified Magic

ISBN 1-888767-28-6, 6x9, softbound, 449 pages,$14.95

"Excellent research manual & workbook...invitingly accessible." - NAPRA ReVIEW

"The book delivers apromised... an important guide for aspiring Qabalists."
- NEW AGE RETAILER

- ♦ Create the magickal body.
- ♦ Open the inner temples of the soul.
- ♦ Create astral doorways through the Qabala.
- ♦ Learn the magickal technique of pathworking.
- ♦ Use the tree of life for divination & initiation.

Entering the Tree of Life
by
Ted Andrews

Spoken Audio
ISBN 1-888767-06-5, 60 Minutes, $10.00 US for Cassette

The music has been composed to facilitate work with any level of the Tree of Life. Side Two provides music and a vocal guidance for experiencing the Temple of Malkuth.

About the Author

Ted Andrews is an internationally recognized author, storyteller, teacher and mystic. A leader in the human potential, metaphysical and psychic field, he has written more than 35 books, which have been translated into twenty-seven foreign languages. He is a popular teacher throughout North America, Europe and parts of Asia.

Ted has been involved in the serious study of the esoteric and the occult for more than 40 years. He has been a certified spiritualist medium for 20 years. He brings to the field an extensive formal and informal education. A former school teacher and counselor, his innovative reading programs received both state and local recognition.

Ted is schooled in music, playing the piano since the age of 12. He also plays bamboo flutes, and he can scratch out a tune or two on the violin/fiddle. He has been a longtime student of sacred dance, ballet and kung fu.

Ted holds state and federal permits to work with birds of prey. He performs wildlife rescue and conducts animal education and storytelling programs with his hawks, owls and other animals in classrooms throughout the year. In his spare time, he hangs out with his menagerie of animals and enjoys horseback riding, ballroom dance and spending time in Nature.

Visit Dragonhawk Publishing online at:
www.dragonhawkpublishing.com

Dragonhawk Publishing   PO Box 10637   Jackson, TN 38308